care
management
series

cms

Leading and Inspiring Teams

Series Editor | Lynda Mason

Andrew Thomas

www.heinemann.co.uk
✓ Free online support
✓ Useful weblinks
✓ 24 hour online ordering

01865 888058

Heinemann

Inspiring generations

Heinemann Educational Publishers
Halley Court, Jordan Hill, Oxford OX2 8EJ
Part of Harcourt Education

Heinemann is the registered trademark of
Harcourt Education Limited

© Andrew Thomas, 2003

Series editor: Lynda Mason

First published 2003

08 07 06 05 04 03
10 9 8 7 6 5 4 3 2 1

British Library Cataloguing in Publication Data is available
from the British Library on request.

ISBN 0 435 45673 3

Designed by Lorraine Inglis
Typeset and illustrated by Tech-Set Ltd, Gateshead
Cover design by Wooden Ark Studio

Printed in the UK by Scotprint Ltd

Cover photo: © Alamy

Acknowledgements
Every effort has been made to contact copyright holders of material reproduced in this book. Any
omissions will be rectified in subsequent printings if notice is given to the publishers.

Tel: 01865 888058 email; info.he@heinemann.co.uk

Contents

Acknowledgements

I would like to thank my family for their unconditional support. Thanks also to Hazel (my 'rock'), my personal editor and lead audio typist who spent every evening, for five months, making sense of my work and for whom nothing is impossible. To my support staff Amy, Dorothy, Tracey, Nicola and Fred who made it all possible.

Thanks to my personal amendment editors, Andrea and Phil Jones, and Christopher Clarke. To my inspirational role model Val Lawrence, to Brian Hawkes, MIOSH, whose expertise within the field of health and safety keeps us all safe. To Rosemary, Christine, Sandra, Lena, Peter and Shelagh whose combined knowledge of library resources knows no bounds. To Terry Wyatt, Roz Milburn, Louise Keeling, Ian Gillings and Ash Das whose knowledge of innovative technology inspires creative application. To my friend and mentor Fred Harvey. To Phillip Orton, Director for Management, and Graham Williams, Director for Care, all the managers, staff and service users at Broad View Care Limited who kindly gave permission for the reproduction of materials as well as a special photo shoot to support this text. Thanks too to Kenneth Grasby, Proprietor, and Nicola Witham, Care Manager, and all the staff and residents of Cordelia Court who gave their valuable time and kind permission for a photo shoot to support this text.

Finally my thanks go to Mary, Matt and Rachel at Heinemann for their continued faith in me.

Photo acknowledgements

The author and publishers would like to thank the following individuals and organisations for their permission to reproduce photographs for this text:

Gareth Bowden – pages 2, 10, 17, 34, 66, 68, 82, 85, 104, 121, 152
Digital Stock – page 144
Rex Features – page 135
Telegraph Colour Library – page 100

Andrew Thomas would also like to thank Broad View Care Limited and Cordelia Court for their kind permisssion to reproduce material in this book.

Introduction

Welcome to *Leading and Inspiring Teams*. This is the second book in the new Heinemann Care Management Series. It combines the knowledge requirements of four essential units for your NVQ 4 Registered Managers Award with the underpinning professional skills required for managing teams effectively.

Person-centred management is one of the most difficult tasks a manager in health or social care will undertake. This text simplifies the rules, the knowledge, the skills and the uncertainties the manager will experience. It explains why teamwork is the most important management tool to deliver care and achieve best practice, irrespective of professional specialism. It is supported by exciting and engaging features, case studies and activities which will reinforce your learning.

About this book

This book contains everything you will need to learn to confidently lead and inspire your team. Underpinning the text are the essential knowledge requirements of the four NVQ 4 units. They are:

RG6	Take responsibility for your business performance and the continuing professional development of self and others.
HSCL4U9	Create, maintain and develop an effective working environment.
C10	Develop teams and individuals to enhance performance.
C13	Manage the performance of teams and individuals.

The structure of the book, which encompasses these key four units, is based on three main chapters. These are:

Chapter 1	Policy and practice
Chapter 2	Tools and techniques
Chapter 3	Achieving best practice

Chapter 1 focuses on current legislative practice which dictates how effective teamwork must conform and respond quickly to changes. Leading and inspiring your team within this context becomes the benchmark for best practice.

Chapter 2 identifies and analyses the tools and techniques that are required to engage in effective teamwork on a multi-disciplinary basis. An understanding of these different mechanisms and tools for application remain a pre-requisite for leading and inspiring your team to engage and sustain effective teamwork practices.

The outcome of leading and inspiring your team is judged on your ability to achieve best practice. Chapter 3 focuses on the means required to achieve realistic and attainable best practice to the highest professional standards demanded of care management.

Features of the book

Throughout the text there are a number of features that are designed to encourage reflection and discussion and to help relate theory to practice. You can also use your written responses to the exercises as evidence towards your NVQ4 Registered Manager Award.

Case studies – examples of real-life situations which will reinforce and consolidate your learning. Questions to check understanding are included which prepare the reader for the unlikely situations that they will face in practice.

What if? – this feature will encourage positive thinking and discussion on how to deal with potentially difficult situations in the workplace.

Reflect on practice – this feature will encourage the reader to reflect on what they are learning in comparison to what actually occurs in the workplace.

A final word

The author involved in the production of this book appreciates the critical importance of developing innovative, realistic and sustainable teamwork practices which can promote team member professional development, and simultaneously deliver qualitative resident care within the practice environment. We hope that this book will help you to achieve this desirable outcome.

Principles and policy

1.1 Data protection

This section concentrates on the need to maintain confidentiality and adhere to the regulations of the Data Protection Act 1998 and the need to maintain confidentiality of data relating to the staff, residents or any other third party, whether in manual or electronic systems. This is a major responsibility for the care manager.

Complying with the law will inspire confidence not only among the work teams but also in your own ability to 'do the job'. Additionally, it is your responsibility to ensure that staff understand they remain both data subjects and data users and at no time must they disclose unauthorised data to a third party, either orally or in writing. Hence there is a clear need for proactive leadership to induct staff into a responsible culture of confidentiality where they can understand their rights, responsibilities and ways of contributing to maintaining data security in the organisation.

In order to gain and retain the confidence of your staff team that any information relating to their individual circumstances remains both secure and confidential, you must:

- induct your staff into a culture of confidentiality that you lead and inspire;
- create a specific data protection policy using the principles of the Data Protection Act 1998;
- ensure staff understand their individual rights and responsibilities to themselves, each other and the organisation.

A culture of confidentiality is a process that is taught, learned and practised. However, what is unique about data protection is that when the three points above are achieved, you will possess a legally binding culture of confidentiality by protecting staff, residents and the organisation irrespective of your type of setting within the care sector. The process begins by understanding the legitimacy and implications of the Data Protection Act 1998, which became legally enforceable on 1 March 2000. The first task is to recognise that this piece of legislation repeals previous Data Protection Acts namely, the Data Protection Act 1984, the Access to Personal Files Act 1987 and the Access to Health Records Act 1990. The 1998 Act, unlike preceding legislation, covers all information (data) of both staff and residents held manually or on computer, with respect to their processing.

The Data Protection Act 1998 covers data held manually and on computer

The data held on team members should include all aspects of employment history, while information on service users should include their initial assessments, care plans and health-related histories. However, the protection of the confidentiality of the above in line with the principles of the Act does pose a major hurdle for those who work both within and outside the care service sector.

The eight principles of the Data Protection Act

Maintaining confidentiality is not a simple matter. The eight principles of the Data Protection Act demand compliance at all times (see Figure 1.1) and it is only through compliance that confidentiality of all identifiable information in relation to service users and staff will be maintained.

All providers of care must now be able to satisfy the legal requirements of retaining and processing information.

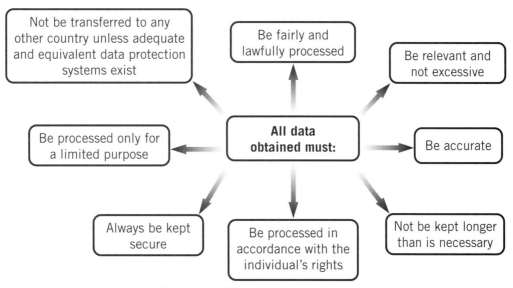

Figure 1.1 The eight principles of the Data Protection Act

Reflect on practice

Are the eight principles of the Data Protection Act recognised, managed and upheld in your practice setting? If not, identify those areas that technically breach this legislation and think about the action required to remedy the situation.

Personal and sensitive information

Each member of staff should have a personal file held manually or in electronic format. The holding of all information – be it on staff or service users, in electronic or paper documents – should adhere to the principles of the Act. This information would normally be broken down into two main areas: personal information and sensitive information

Personal information

- Name
- Address
- Contact telephone number or emergency contact number

Sensitive information

- Age
- National Insurance number and tax code
- Health-related history, including mental health
- Racial or ethnic origin
- Religious beliefs
- Marital status
- Trade union membership (as defined by the Trade Union and Labour Relations Consolidation Act 1992)
- Criminal history

Sensitive information must be subject to stricter conditions of both security and processing. The organisation must have written consent from the Criminal Records Register to hold this information on file and thereby process both personal and sensitive information.

Staff are likely to ask questions about the degree of security that they can expect to ensure the confidential handling and storage of information they have given consent to be processed. Where an electronic system exists, staff will be given a personalised email address to ensure they can view their own individual electronic files to always validate authenticity.

Caldicott guardians and the six Caldicott principles

You must decide whether to take sole responsibility for the security of all staff identifiable information or whether to appoint another senior member of staff to undertake this key role, often referred to as either the data protection officer or the Caldicott guardian.

The Caldicott guardian and an associated set of Caldicott principles originate from a government report published in 1997 that had emanated from a committee chaired by Dame Fiona Caldicott. This report in its original brief focused on patient identifiable information within the National Health Service and made a number of recommendations as to how it should be processed. However, it became obvious that the recommendations, when turned into principles, were sufficiently eclectic to be employed in all work settings. It also became clear that the role of the Caldicott guardian, a person made responsible for both patient information and the maintenance of the confidentiality of the system, could be transplanted within the care service sector, in the same role for staff and service users.

Adherence to the six Caldicott principles represents best practice in the preservation of confidentiality of staff identifiable information as well as residents or any significant third-party interests (see Figure 1.2).

Principle 1 – Focus on purpose
The Caldicott guardian has to justify the use or transfer of any staff identifiable information for any purpose. Rules must be laid down to stipulate what is justifiable in terms of the use or transfer, irrespective of the purpose, and the consent of the staff member must be obtained before any transfer of information.

Principle 2 – Staff identifiable information should not be used unless necessary
Staff identifiable information should not be used unless absolutely necessary and then only with strict controls.

Principle 3 – Ensure time reduction of staff identifiable information
Any use of staff identifiable information must be made only in justifiable circumstances. Clearly, where there is no need to use staff details, do not expose your staff member's identity to a third party.

Principle 4 – Access
Only authorised persons should be allowed access to staff identifiable information and should have access only to items they really need to see and no other.

Principle 5 – Responsibilities
The Caldicott guardian must ensure that the Caldicott principles are understood by all staff members. These must be supervised and monitored to ensure that staff confidentiality becomes a collective responsibility that each person subscribes to.

Principle 6 – Compliance with the law
The Caldicott guardian must at all times ensure that any use of staff identifiable information must conform to statute. Equally, the guardian must ensure that the entire organisation (the practice setting) complies with the law in this respect.

Figure 1.2 The six Caldicott principles

Reflect on practice

How do you employ the six Caldicott principles to protect staff identifiable information within your practice setting? Give examples.

What if...?

If you appointed a Caldicott guardian within your practice setting to operationalise all six Caldicott principles, how could you monitor the results in the short, medium and long term?

CASE STUDY — Caldicott guardian

You manage a large community care agency that works in partnership with local social services departments, local primary health care trusts as well as private and independent providers. You offer full-time home care. You currently employ some 150 staff, who work flexible hours to meet the different needs of service users. To comply with the principles of the Data Protection Act 1998 you will need to appoint a Caldicott guardian. This position you anticipate will be shared between two of your community care managers. Their role will be to record, store and retrieve information, which they must both access and protect.

- What kinds of skills and qualities should a guardian possess to occupy this sensitive yet key role?
- What different kinds of training might you consider to ensure that they can record, store and retrieve information in a confidential manner?
- What methods of supervision of your Caldicott guardians should you consider to ensure your data protection system both complies with the law and protects your staff confidentiality?
- What additional roles might your Caldicott guardians adopt to develop your data protection system? Give examples drawn from your practice setting.

Storing and handling confidential information

Having appointed your Caldicott guardian, your next priority must be how to store staff data safely, in a manner which preserves staff confidence in your data protection system. In practical terms, manual files must be kept within secure, lockable filing cabinets.

Each staff file must be named and retained in a separate lever arch file or secure hanging file. Only the Caldicott guardian or authorised 'others' should be allowed access to information they might require; it is important that anyone accessing information can justify this. Cabinets today can be electronically secured with access codes, which would be made known only to your Caldicott guardian.

Thought must be given to how to maximise the security of the storage environment. A lockable room adjacent to a central office might offer the ideal solution. Information held on CD-ROM might be held in similar accommodation, with each file given a unique password known only to your Caldicott guardian or other authorised persons. Furthermore, this form of storage requires less space, is more practical and is far more secure than its manual counterpart.

Only authorised persons should be allowed to access confidential information

Confidence in the organisation's data protection system is an intrinsic part of leading and inspiring your staff team. Personal ownership of this process ensures a secure collective culture where different methods can operate side by side without inhibition or unnecessary confusion. Practical, user friendly and cost-effective methods of maximising the security of identifiable data are set out in Chapter 2, section 2.3 (see pages 71–6).

CASE STUDY — Record and store staff data legally

You are a manager of a 46-bed private residential home that combines with a day care unit that accommodates up to 30 residents on any one day. You have protected and secured all service user identifiable information under the terms of the Data Protection Act 1998. However, you realise you have not made similar provision to protect confidential staff data. How will you proceed to comply with the law?

- Will you appoint a Caldicott guardian? If so, why?
- How will you put the six Caldicott principles into practice?
- What training might you offer to your Caldicott guardian?
- What methods of information storage might you consider to protect staff confidentiality?
- How will you protect access as well as ensure access to staff to their own information without compromising third-party interests, as required by Standard 14.5 of the Care Standards Act 2000?
- How will you ensure that access and use are justifiable by law in relation to all staff information held on manual or computerised systems?
- What methods might you consider to encourage a collective culture of confidentiality?

Developing a data protection policy

As part of the induction of your staff into an organisational, dynamic culture of confidentiality they must be encouraged to become aware of their rights and, furthermore, how to access their individual data, as well as their responsibilities to themselves, each other and to their organisation. Only then can they be satisfied that their private information is both secure and confidential. This simple task is inspirational in itself and can be achieved by developing and writing a data protection policy which all staff can access, follow and collectively own. An example of a data protection policy is given in Appendix 1.1. Such a policy can be personally distributed to all staff members for private reading. It can then be the subject of further and systematic team training, team briefings, supervision and appraisal to ensure competence and compliance with the law.

Reflect on practice ••

Consider the legal requirements of the Data Protection Act 1998. Then consider the advantages and disadvantages of initiating a data protection policy within your practice setting.

What if...?
If an accidental disclosure of staff personal data was made within your practice setting, even though you already possess a data protection policy, what reasonable measures might you undertake to resolve the situation and demonstrate legal compliance to the principles of the Data Protection Act, to avoid any criminal repercussions?

1.2 Health and safety legislation

This section focuses upon health and safety legislation and its interrelationship with both procedure and practice within the generic care sector. The section begins by examining some of the most relevant questions asked before the development of a policy and procedures as a means of raising staff awareness and understanding of basic health and safety.

Direct reference is made to the Health and Safety at Work Act 1974, as this is seen as the foundation Act in British health and safety law. Further subsidiary regulations or statutory instruments (SIs) by which EU Directives are implemented to further workplace safety are also included in the discussions.

An exemplar of a procedural pathway is developed below to demonstrate those procedures that are required to guide and inform a health and safety policy for actual practice, irrespective of the care setting. With the procedures in place, a health and safety policy focusing on a residential care home for older people is drawn up as an example. The detail demonstrates the diverse content – a statement of intention and comprehensive arrangements for the management of health and safety – to safeguard working conditions and workplace security for residents, staff and other significant parties, in unison and in law. Appendix 1.2 gives an example of a health and safety policy.

Preliminary considerations

Before you attempt to write your health and safety procedures and policy, there are certain searching questions you should ask yourself as a manager and in terms of your team. They include:

- What is a health and safety policy statement?
- Why do you need a health and safety policy statement?
- Whose responsibility is it?
- What arrangements should be described?
- When should policy statements be changed?
- What duties are involved?

What is a health and safety policy statement?

Your health and safety policy statement sets out how you intend to manage health and safety in your organisation. The document must demonstrate who does what, and when and how they will perform the duty.

Why do you need a health and safety policy statement?

The Health and Safety at Work Act 1974, section 2(3), requires any organisation employing five or more people to have in place a written health and safety policy. This is more than just a legal document: it represents the employer's commitment to reasonable and responsible planning and management of health and safety at work. It is quite simply not an option to ignore this.

Whose responsibility is it?

The responsibility for health and safety rests with the owner/manager and the management team, who are classed as 'the employer'. Clearly, it needs to be recognised that many tasks will have to be delegated. Therefore your statement must show how these tasks are allocated. Consultation is the key: your team must be consulted about health and safety issues. They must then be obliged to read, understand and operationalise the policy statement in practice. The policy statement must outline who is responsible for reporting an accident or giving first aid in an emergency.

What arrangements should be described?

You must ensure your policy statement describes the procedures you have in place for ensuring the health and safety of all service users, visitors and team members. Additionally, all your staff, irrespective of status, must have personal access to the policy statement.

Your health and safety policy should be accessible to team members, service users and visitors

When should policy statements be changed?

Changes are usually required as a result of organisational and legislative change that demands amendment to actual practice. Therefore it is considered best practice to review your policy regularly, perhaps every six months, and sooner if needs dictate.

What duties are involved?

A whole range of duties will need to be carried out, including duties that relate to other relevant legislation. For example, the Management of Health and Safety at Work Regulations 1999 demand that you assess and grade all risks emanating from work-related duties and subsequently record your findings. Given the diversity of the generic care sector, other legislation will apply, such as the Health and Safety First Aid Regulations 1981, the Reporting of Injuries, Diseases and Dangerous Occurrences Regulations (RIDDOR) 1995, the Manual Handling Operations Regulations 1992 and the Control of Substances Hazardous to Health Regulations (COSHH) 2002 (see Figure 1.3). What you write in your policy has to be put into practice, evidenced in writing and then internally and externally monitored by both the National Care Commissioners and the Health & Safety Executive.

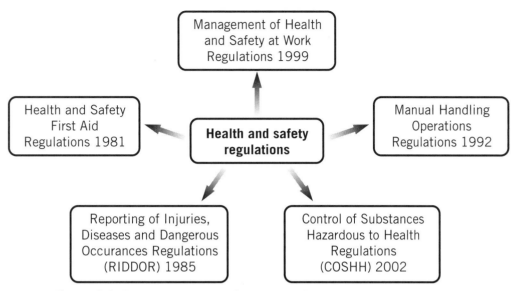

Figure 1.3 The health and safety regulations that you will need to consider

Developing a policy

The obvious starting point would be the Health and Safety at Work Act 1974 (HASAWA) as it covers all staff and obliges all employers to provide safe arrangements for working and by outcome a safe place of work. The Act also carries a duty of care, which is a two-way arrangement between employer and employee. This requires all staff to undertake personal care of their own health and safety and to cooperate with their employer in facilitating all policies and procedures relating to health and safety matters.

Each workplace with more than five workers must have in place a written statement of the health and safety policy. This policy must include:

- a statement of the policy's intention to provide a safe and healthy workplace;
- the name of the person responsible for its implementation;
- the names of the management team responsible for carrying out the policy;
- a system for recording all workplace accidents;
- fire evacuation procedures.

The Health and Safety at Work Act 1974 became an enabling piece of legislation within the context of British health and safety law. It specifies, for the first time, not only the duties that employers have towards employees but also the responsibilities that employees have to themselves and to one another. The health and social care sectors are covered by this Act and its requirements. Naturally, over time the Act has been amended and new subsidiary regulations and statutory instruments have been introduced by which EU Directives have been implemented. These have affected every care setting.

What if...?

If a health and safety inspector made a spot check on your care setting and asked to see your health and safety policy, would you know where to locate it? Would you be able to satisfy the inspector of its contents in relation to your organisational practice? If not, what action do you need to take?

Workplace procedures to be included in the policy

The procedures you put in place should be both reasonable and practicable to ensure healthy and safe working conditions, equipment and systems of operation for all your team members. Equally, your procedures should both inform and guide your writing of the health and safety policy, together with any revisions you may need to make to ensure it remains within the law.

On a cautionary note, what you write in the policy has to be put into practice. The final test of a health and safety policy is not how eloquently it is written but how safe the conditions are within the workplace.

To demonstrate the workplace procedures required to meet Care Standard 38.4 of the Care Standards Act 2000, together with the related health and safety legislation, a procedural pathway is given in Table 1.1 as an exemplar. This is a good starting point or source of reference. It lists those procedures that are required as a minimum standard.

Table 1.1 The procedural pathway

1	*Statement of intention, statement of general policy*	These statements should be signed and dated by the owner, managing director, or person responsible.
2	*Responsibilities, day-to-day activities and specific areas of work*	This is a tripartite procedure, as it must link in with your procedures for: competency for tasks and training; accidents, first aid and work-related ill-health; and monitoring.
3	*Health and safety risks arising from work-based activities*	Identify the risks, make the decisions required to eradicate them, and ensure appropriate control of the process. Ensure there is a named person for this activity and an adequate timescale for action. Set, in advance, the times for formal review. This should provide a procedural function to the facilitation of Manual Handling Operations Regulations 1992, the Management of Health and Safety at Work Regulations 1992/1999 as well as COSHH 2002. It also relates to the management of safe plant and equipment and safe handling and use of substances.
4	*Consultation with employees.*	Identify a named person to undertake the consultation process. Identify employee representatives for feedback from staff to ensure that they can effectively communicate potential hazards which may cause injury or harm. This is particularly important if your organisation is large. It links in with the Consultation Regulations 1996 and the Safety Representative Regulations 1997.

5	*Safe plant and equipment*	A named person must be responsible for essential maintenance. This person should then decide how regular maintenance needs to be, is responsible for drafting maintenance procedures and is the person other staff report to if problems arise. Additionally, you must decide who is responsible for the purchasing of new plant and equipment, and who should sanction the purchase and why. These procedures link with the Provision and Use of Work Equipment Regulations 1998. There is a further link to your procedures to manage health and safety risks arising from work-related activities.
6	*Safe handling and use of hazardous substances*	A named person must be responsible for identifying and recording hazardous substances. Identify and appoint a person to undertake the COSHH assessments required; this process informs employees, allows for monitoring of work and should assist any review assessments undertaken. This relates to your procedure on health and safety risks arising from a particular area of work.
7	*Information, supervision and induction*	Who is responsible for the display of health and safety law posters and who might be responsible for the issue of information leaflets and the like? All signs used have to be in pictogram colour: for example, green and white indicates safe; red and white indicates prohibited; blue and white indicates mandatory; yellow and black indicates hazards. Who trains new recruits and supervises their progression and who is responsible for the maintenance and safe keeping of records? Training: identify named person(s) responsible for induction training, additional mentoring and who retains training and progressional records. In order to ensure a procedure, which realises competency, it remains vital that specific knowledge, learning outcomes and evidence requirements are put in place, monitored and reviewed. This procedure links into the responsibilities of your management structure.
8	*Accidents at work and first aid*	Identify the named person who keeps records on health related surveillance and the appointed first-aiders, and who arranges training and retraining every three years. Who is responsible for purchasing, maintaining and monitoring the use of first aid equipment? Who is responsible for reporting under the RIDDOR 1995? This links in with procedure for managing and minimising health and safety risks arising from any work-related activity.
9	*Fire and emergency evacuation procedures*	Who is the named person responsible for undertaking fire risk assessments? Who has responsibility for the testing of fire extinguishers, alarms, escape routes and safe evacuation procedures? Who takes responsibility to ensure that all staff, service users, visitors and members of the public are aware of the evacuation procedures? Who monitors and reviews these procedures and liaises with the local fire brigade to ensure they remain realistic and lawful?

10	*Monitoring and reviewing*	Who monitors and reviews, on a regular basis, safe working practices? Who takes responsibility for the supervision and review of risk assessments, safety policy, annual COSSH assessments and for the investigation of work-related accidents, sickness and stress? This procedure underpins your responsibility to manage and monitor everyday work activities within your practice setting.

CASE STUDY – Revision of procedures

As the owner of a 40-bed residential home for older people, you have become increasingly aware of the lack of procedural detail to guide your staff in their work. To comply with the Health and Safety at Work Act 1974 and subsidiary legislation, an overhaul of all your procedures becomes an urgent requirement to maintain a safe and healthy working environment. How do you proceed?

- Give examples of where your procedures might omit information or fail to designate responsibility.
- What methods could you use to consult your staff representatives and how much would you empower them to contribute towards procedural revision?
- How will you monitor changes to existing procedures to ensure safe working practices?
- What systems of recording might you employ?
- On what basis would you delegate to named persons to identify and record hazardous substances as well as to undertake COSHH 2002 assessments?
- How will you ensure that any procedural revision influences your home's health and safety policy? Consider the changes of arrangements you will require and re-list to maintain a safe working environment according to statute.

Reflect on practice

Consider how your organisation differentiates between the costs and benefits of having an effective and monitored health and safety policy.

CASE STUDY – Improved fire evacuation procedures

You are a care manager of a 23-bed, single-storey residential home for older persons. Fire prevention and safe evacuation have always featured prominently in the home's health and safety policy. Following ongoing assistance from the advisory unit of your local fire brigade, as well as your attached social care commissioner, successive fire drills once a fortnight had achieved complete and safe evacuation within six minutes. More recently you have accommodated three new residents with mobility needs. Subsequently the last fire drill achieved safe evacuation in nine minutes.

- How do you restore your optimum time of six minutes without placing your residents and staff at greater risk?
- Could you seek expert advice from your local fire brigade inspection unit and your attached social care commissioner? Why might you do so?
- What reasonable arrangements might you make to improve your current evacuation procedures?
- What methods of consultation with all your staff teams will you employ?
- How could establishing an informed culture of safe evacuation for residents and staff speed up the evacuation process?
- Give examples of the physical aids you might employ.
- What monitoring methods might you employ to ensure reduced timescales of safe evacuation are maintained? Give examples that could satisfy external inspection.

CASE STUDY — Review of risk assessment in relation to safe manual handling techniques

You are a manger of a 46-bed nursing home for older dependent persons. Many of your residents experience multiple disabilities and complex medical conditions. A high proportion of residents requires short-term one-to-one care. A recent review of the establishment's 'no lifting' policy showed that some staff were taking inappropriate risks and not using the equipment provided, particularly hoists to lift the residents safely. You need to take urgent action to raise staff awareness of and compliance with the no lifting policy, and to consider the Manual Handling Operations Regulations 1992 as well as advice from the Health & Safety Executive in relation to proper risk assessment when undertaking manual handling.

- How could you encourage a new culture in which staff themselves identify potential hazards in relation to manual handling?
- What types of written instruction might you prepare?
- How might you involve all staff and safety representatives in the process?
- How might staff be guided to avoid harm at all costs?
- How could you encourage staff always to evaluate the risks of their actions and encourage a culture where everyone considers existing precautions and makes a judgement of adequacy on whether more should be done to avoid injury?
- How might you encourage individual and team-based evaluation of everyday risks?
- What methods of recording currently exist? Could they be improved to minimise risk while respecting resident confidentiality? Is your duty of care under the Health and Safety at Work Act 1974 compromised by the strict requirements of resident confidentiality, under the Data Protection Act 1998? How do you reasonably and practically overcome this?
- How could you encourage your staff individually and in teams regularly to review their own assessments of risk and revise work practice?

1.3   Equal opportunities legislation and its relationship to work, training and development

This section focuses upon how equal opportunities legislation facilitates equal access to work, training and development. A case is made for equal opportunities being a philosophy for all staff in the generic care sector, through a common value base and the interrelationship between policy and procedure. Procedure is the vehicle necessary for promoting equality within a generic care team, and thus enabling best practice to occur.

This section also includes an examination of discrimination in employment, training and development. A detailed descriptive analysis of the various legislation that exists is included to demonstrate how it can, when collectively used, minimise the incidence of discrimination.

A procedural exemplar of how, in practice, you can promote equality of opportunity in employment, training and development, is given in Appendix 1.3.

Equal opportunities values

Every practice setting which seeks to employ, train and develop its staff must support the principles of equality of opportunity and must subscribe to its underpinning legislation. Furthermore, the care sector possesses a philosophy of core values, which it must endeavour both to practise and to share with service users and staff, without prejudice.

The care value base

The core values of the care sector relate to acceptance of and respect for the individual, personal autonomy, confidentiality and non-condemnation. Collectively they form the basis of how care is practised on either an individual or multidisciplinary basis. By implication they should be endorsed in every aspect of service delivery, to ensure that staff and service users realise their full potential. On this basis, then, equal opportunities is a philosophy for everyone, particularly in relation to employment, training and continuous development.

Therefore, as a manager, a necessary part of leading and inspiring your team is to ensure that equality of opportunity is both policy and procedure – tangible and understood by everyone. In reality, this means that both policy and procedure become interrelated and the latter becomes the vehicle by which equality and best practice are promoted.

Reflect on practice •

How does the practice of equal opportunities operate within your establishment?

Equality of opportunity is a philosophy for everyone working in the care sector

Discrimination

As manager, in relation to the employment, training and development of your staff, you should be aware of those grounds on which it is unlawful to discriminate (see Figure 1.4).

In this connection, it is unlawful for an employer to inhibit or intrude upon an employee's or applicant's family life and privacy. The section above on data protection and the disclosure of sensitive and identifiable information is also relevant here.

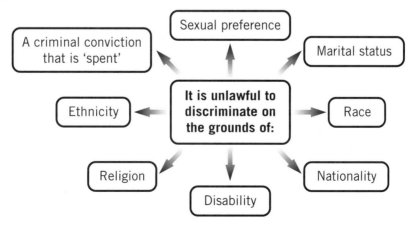

Figure 1.4 Unlawful discrimination

Supporting legislation to minimise discrimination

Since the early 1970s there has been a battery of legislation passed to protect basic rights and responsibilities, in particular of disadvantaged groups. However, it has become clear that no amount of legislation will prevent discrimination unless there is a collective will by all concerned both to challenge and, if necessary, to prosecute. So, how can legislation help and what do you need to understand and translate into practice? A good understanding of the following legislation should ensure the level of knowledge required to enable competence in dealing with any issues that may arise.

EQUAL PAY ACT 1970

The primary objective of this Act is to ensure that women receive the same pay and treatment as men in similar employment. Pay is defined under the Act to include sick pay and redundancy payments. Therefore the work of women must be given equal value to that of men. Under the Act, women must have:

- an equivalent rate of pay;
- the same rights as men to join a pension scheme;
- the same fringe benefits, such as subsidised meals and additional holidays in lieu of service.

In order for a claim for pay discrimination to be valid, the comparison must be made to a man or woman in the same or similar employment, by the same employer, or affiliated employer.

SEX DISCRIMINATION ACT 1975

This Act makes discrimination on grounds of sex, either direct or indirect, unlawful. This is of particular importance when addressing the whole process of employment, training and staff development.

RACE RELATIONS ACT 1976/2000

The Act makes discrimination on the grounds of race, ethnicity or national origin, be it direct or indirect, unlawful. Akin to the Sex Discrimination Act 1975, the Race Relations Act 1976 refers to direct and indirect discrimination and serves to protect the rights of staff, be they full time, part time or on temporary contract. It also protects clients.

Direct discrimination means treating an individual, in terms of employment, training and staff development, less favourably than another, for example because of their gender, race, disability or marital status. A typical example of discrimination would be if a black man applied for a job as care manager and was advised at interview that he would not fit in with the values of an all-white staff and resident group.

Indirect discrimination arises when the requirements for a job disadvantage a minority group. An example might be a traditional Hindu woman who applies for a job as a residential care enabler for people with learning disabilities. At interview, she is told she would have to comply with casual dress requirements. Such a demand could be in conflict with her cultural requirements and as such indirectly compromise her application. This would be illegal.

REHABILITATION OF OFFENDERS ACT 1974

This Act facilitates the rehabilitation of people who have previously offended and received a sentence of 30 months or less, after their conviction(s) are termed as 'spent'. The nature of the conviction and the age of the offender will determine the time before the conviction is considered spent. The Rehabilitation of Offenders Act declaration is required to be signed by offenders with a background of consistent crime against individuals. However, those vulnerable groups such as older people, children and people with disabilities are protected by the National Police Register, which monitors the movement and rehabilitation of previous offenders. Nevertheless, as care manager you need to be aware that it is illegal to discriminate on the grounds of a spent conviction.

DISABILITY DISCRIMINATION ACT 1995

This Act gives individuals classified as disabled the right not to be discriminated against without justifiable reason. Moreover, employers must make reasonable adjustments to premises to enable a disabled person to occupy a role for which he or she is qualified. As care manager, you need to be vigilant not to discriminate against a disabled person during employment, recruitment, training and development processes.

ASYLUM AND IMMIGRATION ACT 1996

Any manager (care or otherwise) employing an individual who does not have permission to work in the United Kingdom on or after 27 January 1997 risks a criminal conviction.

DATA PROTECTION ACT 1998

Information received and held on all team members must be recognised as identifiable, personal, sensitive and therefore protected as confidential. All records relating to personal details, training, supervision, appraisal and records of achievement must be retained within safe environments and secure accommodation.

Only information that is current and relevant should be retained and then must be held no longer than is necessary. Any destruction of information must comply with the provisions of the Act. Furthermore, no information relating to personnel must be transferred to other areas of your organisation without permission.

HUMAN RIGHTS ACT 1998

Guidance from government stipulates that employers must ensure that basic human rights are respected and reflected in day-to-day work. In relation to employment, training and staff development, this can include:

- employment policies and recruitment criteria;
- training plans and contracts for progression;
- staff development policies, training profiles together with supervision and appraisal contracts and records;
- the way such work is organised and managed;
- demonstrations and evidence to show how decisions are reached and that respect for human rights is shown throughout the process.

Care Standards Act 2000

The National Minimum Standards for Care, defined in the Care Standards Act 2000, identify the core requirements for all care homes providing personal or nursing care to older people. As care manager, you must be conversant with the standards as they apply to your setting. In particular:

- Standards 17.1–17.3 demand that service users' legal rights are protected.
- Standards 18.1–18.6 demand that service users are protected from abuse.
- Standards 27.1–27.7 demand that the numbers and skill mix of staff meets service users' needs.
- Standards 28.1–28.3 demand that service users are in safe hands at all times.
- Standards 29.1–29.6 demand that service users are supported and protected by the home's recruitment policy and practices.
- Standards 30.1–30.4 demand that all staff are trained and competent to do their jobs.

This Act, which became law on 1 April 2002, makes it essential that appropriate policies and procedures are drawn up, specifically in relation to employment, training and staff development. It is a priority for any manager to have the policies and procedures properly documented, to show evidence of equality of opportunity. Additionally, all practice must be sufficiently transparent to undergo external inspection via the National Social Care Commissioners, who will monitor the implementation of this Act.

Reflect on practice

Consider how legislation affects procedures relating to employment, training and staff development in your practice setting. Decide whether you think there are possible omissions and what possible legislative redress could be made.

CASE STUDY — Ensuring legislative equality

You are a regional care manager of a national charity which provides residential and community care to people with a learning disability. The organisation has always striven to promote equality of opportunity within both service delivery and staffing. An equal opportunities policy was written some 15 years ago but has not been updated. In the light of successive legislation you realise that a new policy must be written. How do you proceed?

- What criteria will you employ to benchmark contents of the previous policy against the new model? Identify your needs in relation to practice and staffing.
- How might you embrace a new culture of equality by incorporating a policy of anti-discrimination? Give examples of what you might include in such a policy.
- How will consultation take place?
- What processes need to be introduced to include the required views and values of residents, service users, staff and the organisation collectively?

● How might you ensure that the future employment, training and continuous staff development of each member of your organisation complies with all relevant statutes and can be evidenced for inspection purposes?

Linking policy and practice

Clearly, policy and procedure are inextricably interrelated and thereby become one when translated into a practice advisory document. It might be reasonably suggested that equality of opportunity in its absolute form is so fluid and dynamic that it becomes outdated as soon as a policy is written.

Constant legislative change, diversity of service users' needs and demands, as well as the requirements under statute to employ, train and develop staff to occupy current and future roles, require organisational change and not simply new policies. As such, a procedural exemplar is given in Appendix 1.3 in accordance with the need to promote equality of opportunity in relation to employment, training and staff development. Within the exemplar all three areas are addressed individually.

Following a procedural framework, such as the one given in Appendix 1.3, will help you to promote equal access to employment, training and ongoing staff development. However, in order that it remains dynamic and reflects best practice, it must be the subject of constant review, monitoring and evaluation. Only then will it cease to be a paper exercise and genuinely assist in facilitating greater equality of opportunity within generic care settings.

1.4 Disciplinary and grievance procedures

The accurate and effective use of legislative procedures is a sure sign of a competent and confident manager. Leading and inspiring staff requires a sound understanding of all aspects of disciplinary and grievance procedures; therefore this section has been written to direct your attention towards the need to have sound organisational disciplinary and grievance procedures in place. Together they represent the care manager's responsibility for ensuring service user and staff safety as well as for maintaining high standards of contractual work performance to inspire the confidence of service users and carers in their purchased care.

As care manager, you need to develop an understanding of how staff discipline relates to proactive teamwork and some of the reasons behind management avoidance, as well as the consequences of not disciplining staff and likely outcomes. Advice is given in this section as to what to avoid when engaging in disciplinary action as well as guidance on two useful methods for disciplinary intervention.

Guidance is provided on how to investigate a disciplinary situation while simultaneously managing the actual process, particularly in relation to disciplinary penalties and the law. An emphasis is given to the need to maintain accurate and confidential records and to supervise the overall process with a view to bringing about necessary and desirable change in staff members' performance.

Additionally, attention is given to the context and management of the grievance procedure, the actual interview and outcome as a means of resolving contested issues at the earliest juncture. Combined management of both areas serves to maintain the continuity and standard of required team performance and care, irrespective of the nature of the practice setting within the care service sector.

 ## What does staff discipline mean?

Staff discipline means different things to different people. For one manager it can mean an informal 'off the cuff chat' while to another it can mean the formal disciplinary process. It is therefore helpful to explore meanings provided by management theorists. For example, the two quotes offered here indicate what the disciplinary process means in practice.

> 'A disciplinary procedure is essentially a series of rules relating to behaviour at work. By establishing rules for minimum acceptable standards of contact an employer is making it clear to employees what is acceptable and what is not. For pragmatic reasons, clear rules ensure consistency and so should indicate what action will be taken if the rules are broken. They should be in writing and clearly communicated to all employees.' (Bedward *et al.*, 1997, p. 305)

> 'Taking disciplinary action is necessarily unpleasant and it is important therefore to establish at the outset precisely who is responsible for enforcing regulations. First, identify the source or the rules. Is there an updated rulebook? If so, are its procedures clearly defined? How should disciplinary incidents be recorded? Note the important distinction between formal and informal warnings when documenting disciplinary events. In law an unrecorded informal warning cannot be used to justify disciplinary action following a repetition of the offence. Informal warnings are precisely that, i.e. off the cuff reminders not to behave in a certain way. Vindication of disciplinary sanctions requires detailed cataloguing of misdemeanours as they occur and the issue of formal written warnings outlining the likely consequences of continuing errant behaviour. Moreover, miscreants must be informed that incidents have been recorded.' (Bennett, 1989, pp. 216–17)

The quotes above suggest that the actual disciplinary process, if managed well, promotes fairness and consistency to the member of staff involved and, indeed, the whole organisation. Therefore, the emphasis needs to be placed on the content of the procedure as well as its impartial use.

The disciplinary process, whether informal or formal, should promote fairness and consistency in the practice setting

Legislative context

The origins of disciplinary action can be traced back to the Industrial Relations Act 1971, which gave prospective employees the opportunity to seek legal redress at an industrial tribunal if they considered they had been unfairly dismissed. The tribunal was renamed the employment tribunal under the Employment Rights Act 1998.

The Industrial Relations Code of Practice (1972) supplemented the 1971 Act, but this was superseded in 1975 by the *Disciplinary Practice and Procedures in Employment*, a Code of Practice produced by the Advisory, Conciliation and Arbitration Service (ACAS). Further legislation followed with the Employment Protection (Consolidation) Act 1978, the Wages Act 1986, the Sunday Trading Act 1994 and the Trade Union Reform and Employment Rights Act 1993 (TURERA). A further Act was passed in 1996 which related directly to discipline and dismissal. Section 3 of this Act specifies in law an employee's right to a statement of employment particulars and furthermore identifies whom employees can appeal to if they are dissatisfied with any disciplinary decisions or actions that are taken. The Employment Rights (Disputes Resolution) Act 1998 provided further protection for employees by facilitating voluntary arbitration in the event of alleged unfair dismissal.

Finally, the Employment Relations Act 1999 was passed with a view to replacing the idea of conflict in the workplace with the concept of partnership, which sought to underline the whole issue of industrial relations law. This Act focuses on rights for the individual, collective bargaining in respect of trade unions and family friendly policies dedicated to maternity/parental leave; it also gives the right to be accompanied at disciplinary and grievance hearings. Furthermore, fairness at work did not mention part-time workers, although in this respect the Part Time Work Directive was passed in 2000.

Avoiding disciplinary action

It is clear from the legislative context that managing discipline and grievance procedures is an important part of any manager's role and yet for many this can be a daunting experience. There would appear to be a range of difficulties attached to the whole area of staff discipline:

- There is the possibility of alienation of a popular manager from the staff group.
- Disciplining a member of staff can cause friction with the wider staff group.
- Staff morale could be undermined, which can have negative effects on service delivery. For example, who is likely to suffer the effects of low staff morale? The service user. To whom do they and their carers complain? The care manager.
- Additional stress from disciplinary action can affect three sides – service users and staff, including the manager.
- The existence of poor staff performance may reflect inadequacies in the manager's own style of practice.
- Disciplining employees, if not legally managed quickly, can escalate into union action, which puts managers in a negative light and undermines their role and authority.

You must ensure that your organisation possesses a disciplinary procedure to guarantee that issues are dealt with quickly and fairly; such a procedure will also set contractual standards of working behaviour. Organisational rules and standards must be maintained to ensure the safety of service users and staff. Furthermore, working performance can be measured against these organisational standards, as can overall service user satisfaction with every aspect of their care and wellbeing.

Reflect on practice

In your experience, what techniques might you or other managers employ to avoid disciplining staff?

Consequences of avoiding staff discipline

In some respects this has already been touched upon, but it is useful to be clear about the possible consequences of avoiding staff discipline issues. The bottom line could well be that the care manager actually loses a job because of poor performance. Aside from this, there would certainly be no respect or opportunities for leading a successful team. Furthermore:

- The avoidance of disciplinary procedures may encourage a culture of poor standards of work performance.
- It may undermine staff, service user and carer morale. Once confidence is lost it is difficult to win back.
- General respect in the care manager's ability to manage could be jeopardised.
- It would almost certainly leave other staff, and more importantly service users, vulnerable to poor practice.

Managing discipline effectively

Clearly, avoidance of disciplinary issues is not acceptable for a good care manager. It would be a far better approach to adopt systems and structures that will allow the confident handling of any situations, should they arise. Two such systems are outlined here: the framework method and the close gap method.

The framework method

This refers to contractual rules which guide work behaviour and would include standards of work and care. Unless you have an agreed framework to start with, you cannot measure whether a member of staff falls below the minimum acceptable level.

The close gap method

This must represent the decisive response. It ensures that both rules and standards are maintained at all times. If a 'gap' occurs between what is expected and what is actually done, then steps need to be taken to close the gap. It is as simple as that. In other words, you must supervise and measure actual performance and determine whether there is any gap between this and what is required. Proactive supervision and observation of practice should be used to identify the actual gaps, which ideally should be closed without the need for formal disciplinary action.

Breaches of rules or standards

Some breaches of rules or standards will not immediately require a formal response from a manager, although they will demand some form of active management intervention. Examples of these breaches would be:

- poor timekeeping;
- persistent absenteeism;
- lifting when there is a 'no lifting' policy;
- not using safety equipment (e.g. hoists) provided by the employer.

Other actions are likely to result in formal disciplinary action. The most common of these include:

- theft or fraud;
- bullying;
- any form of physical violence;
- negligence that either leads to or has the potential to lead to injury, death or damage to property;
- deliberate damage to organisational or service user property;
- drug or alcohol abuse while on duty;
- infringement of health and safety rules;
- bringing the organisation into disrepute.

Developing a disciplinary policy

In its advisory handbook *Discipline at Work*, which includes a revised Code of Practice, ACAS has identified 14 essential features of a disciplinary procedure (ACAS, 2000, paragraph 9, pp. 59–60).

A disciplinary procedure must:
- be in writing;
- specify to whom it applies;
- be non-discriminatory;
- provide for matters to be dealt with without undue delay;
- provide for proceedings, witness statements and records to be kept confidential;
- indicate the disciplinary actions which may be taken;
- specify the levels of management which have the authority to take the various forms of disciplinary action;
- provide for workers to be informed of the complaints against them and where possible all relevant evidence before any hearing;
- provide workers with an opportunity to state their case before decisions are reached;
- provide workers with the right to be accompanied (see also section 3 of the revised ACAS Code of Practice 2000 for information on the statutory right to be accompanied);
- ensure that, except for gross misconduct, no worker is dismissed for a first breach of discipline;
- ensure that disciplinary action is not taken until the case has been fully investigated;
- ensure that workers are given an explanation for any penalty imposed;
- provide a right of appeal – normally to a more senior manager – and specify the procedure to be followed.

(Reproduced with kind permission of The Stationery Office)

Having identified the main points a disciplinary procedure should contain, you must ensure that a disciplinary procedure exists for the organisation, ideally one that reflects the features of good practice listed by ACAS. Examples of a disciplinary procedure/policy for any organisation are given in Appendix 1.4 and Appendix 1.5.

In addition to the formal written policy, you should observe the following points when dealing with disciplinary issues:

- Do not rely on hearsay or gossip – stick to evidenced facts.
- Never humiliate a member of staff in public, that is, before other staff, service users or their carers.
- The care manager must not be seen to bear grudges.
- Do not employ group pressure to scapegoat someone.
- Do not use unrealistic threats that cannot be supported by company, trust or departmental policy.
- Do not make the situation public knowledge.
- Do not judge simply using personality traits without factual evidence.
- It is always inadvisable to act spontaneously.
- Do not hide the possible consequences of the action being pursued.
- Remember that the person who is subject to a disciplinary procedure has the right to present their own account of the alleged events.
- Above all, do not abuse the principles of confidentiality, which the disciplinary process demands.

What if...?

Consider any other actions relevant to your own experience of work that a care manager must not do when faced with a situation of potential/actual disciplinary action. Share your responses with peers and list them in order of priority.

The disciplinary process is there to protect service users and staff, and to prevent contractual rules being broken and standards of performance dropping. It must also support improvement in unsatisfactory performance before it results in more serious consequences for both the staff member and the organisation.

In the event of action that requires disciplinary procedures, you must follow the disciplinary process laid down. It should cover:

- investigation of events;
- the disciplinary interview;
- a decision regarding a penalty;
- feedback to the member of staff;
- appeal.

These are discussed under separate headings below.

The investigation of events and preparations for the disciplinary interview

There are some procedures and rules that can be followed when investigating the events that are alleged to have taken place. Following these will help to ensure best practice at all times. For example:

- Relevant facts relating to the event must be recorded. This will require you to take statements from service users, staff and carers or any other person involved. Statements must be factual and thorough. Therefore care and time must be spent to ensure accuracy, as these records will represent vital evidence of what has occurred.

- Ensure that the person who is being disciplined is informed of what the process consists of and the length of time likely to be required to perform the investigation. Depending on the seriousness of the allegation or offence, it might become necessary to suspend the staff member on full pay while an investigation is undertaken. An example of a letter giving notice of suspension from work is given in Appendix 1.6. However, this needs to be explained only as an option if required as part of the overall disciplinary process. An example of a letter giving notice of a disciplinary hearing is given in Appendix 1.7.

- Inform the staff member of the nature of the allegation, employees' rights under the disciplinary procedure, and the requirement to attend the disciplinary interview. Remind the staff member there is a right to be represented at the interview.

- Consider the staff member's personal explanation for what has happened and investigate appropriately.

- Give the staff member appropriate time to prepare a case, ideally to a mutually negotiated timescale.

- Arrange a suitable venue, which ensures maximum confidentiality and minimum interruption.

- Make sure you have all the evidence to hand.

- Ensure appropriate time is available for the interview.

- Delegate a second member of senior staff to be present, both to witness the proceedings and to take notes.

- If there are witnesses who are required to attend the interview ensure that they can attend or a substitute witness statement is made and accepted in advance by the staff member.

- If language presents a problem, consider the employment of a suitable interpreter.

- Check what disciplinary action has been taken in the past for similar actions.

- Ensure that the staff member's disciplinary record is checked beforehand.

Reflect on practice

Review the rules for preparing for a disciplinary interview within your organisation. Compare them with those presented here. What improvements could be made to ensure good practice?

Managing the disciplinary interview

There are several stages involved in managing the disciplinary interview.

Introduction and scene setting

It is important to introduce the staff member to everyone present (this might include a third party such as a trade union representative, colleague or friend) and remind him or her why the interview is taking place. It will be important to ensure that the staff member is aware that the interview is part of the organisation's disciplinary procedure for all contractual staff.

You should then explain to the staff member both the content and the purpose of the interview. You must outline the precise nature of the complaint and share with the staff member, and representative, if present, any written statements made by witnesses and ensure understanding.

Hearing the evidence

Once the introduction and scene setting are completed, allow the staff member to state his or her case, present any evidence or have the opportunity to call witnesses in defence, if necessary. It is useful to remember two points:

- Always ask open-ended questions which require a substantial reply. Use closed questions only when confirmation is required.
- Always keep calm, be polite and listen actively to ensure the staff member feels sufficiently at ease to discuss all matters freely.

Take notes or delegate this task. If for any reason there is no supporting evidence for the allegations made, the proceeding must be stopped and appropriate apologies made to the staff member. However, on the other hand, if new evidence comes to light as a result of the interview and an extension to the investigation is required, then an adjournment to a set time scale must be made and agreed.

Delegate a second member of staff to be present, both to witness the proceedings and to take notes

Summarising the events

In most cases, if the interview runs its course, it is good practice to summarise the major points raised. Ensure that the staff member understands all the issues involved and check to make sure that no area or information has been omitted and that fairness is seen to be practised.

Deciding the outcome

Before making a final decision based on the facts presented, particularly if a penalty is to be imposed, it is considered good practice to adjourn the interview to review all areas raised and make sure they will be addressed. This is to ensure that all areas of the process have been adhered to. If appropriate, cross-check any evidence presented via a further investigation and ensure there is no conflicting evidence that casts doubt on the allegation made. It may also be necessary to check the staff member's current work record for similar past instances or allegations made or not supported against present members of staff. Finally, question whether the disciplinary interview supports the use of any penalty to be imposed and consider whether a penalty is actually reasonable and fair given the presenting facts.

On a cautionary note, it is imperative that the management of the disciplinary interview remains a transparent and fair process. In this way the process ceases to be punitive and is more likely to create a culture of respect for rules and regulations. This becomes a formidable tool in winning the trust and support of team members, which is what leading and inspiring teams is all about.

 # Disciplinary penalties available

Oral warning

In the instance of a minor offence, which is upheld, the staff member should be given a formal oral warning. The staff member must be informed that it will be held on the contractual personal record for a specified period of time (e.g. six months) and then disregarded if no further breaches are made.

First formal written warning

If the offence falls into a more serious category, then a first formal written warning may be given. An example of such a letter is given in Appendix 1.8. Again, the staff member must be informed that it will be retained on the personal file for a specified time (e.g. 8 or 12 months) and then disregarded on provision that no further breaches are made. This penalty should also serve to reinforce to the staff member that a final written warning would be considered if no improvement in actual working performance is made.

Final written warning

If the staff member had already received a previous warning for poor performance or misconduct, then a final written warning can be sustained. Additionally, such a warning might be used in instances of a 'first offence' considered serious but not sufficient to support dismissal. Again, the staff member must be informed that it will remain on his or her personal file for a specified time (e.g. 12 months). It is quite common to include a written statement within this warning that any further evidence of misconduct may lead to dismissal.

Sanctions short of dismissal

If the staff member has already received a final written warning, further misconduct not so serious to justify dismissal might lead to the imposition of sanctions, such as:

- disciplinary suspension without pay;
- disciplinary transfer;
- demotion;
- loss of increment benefit;
- loss of post.

It is important to emphasise that contracts of employment allow for the imposition of those penalties and staff be informed of such outcomes.

Dismissal

If the staff member's performance has not improved within the specified time scale, despite warnings, dismissal is the final step to be taken. Unless the staff member is being dismissed for evidenced misconduct, he or she is entitled by law to a period of notice or payment in lieu of notice. The booklet *Rights to Notice and Reasons for Dismissal* (Department of Trade and Industry, 2002) is freely available to both staff and employer for further guidance. Appendix 1.9 gives an example of a letter terminating employment.

Dismissal without notice

Dismissal without notice is undertaken only when the type of serious misconduct destroys contractual arrangements and so makes any type of normative working relationship impossible. This type of dismissal (i.e. without a contractual period of notice or pay in lieu of notice) is restricted to very serious offences such as theft or physical violence. Dismissal without notice (or any dismissal, for that matter) for misconduct must follow the usual procedure of investigation, informing and interviewing the staff member with representation (if he or she chooses) and establishing the facts.

Official feedback to the staff member following the disciplinary interview

Following the disciplinary interview and the review of the situation, the staff member and any representative must be informed orally of the sanctions and given the facts underpinning a decision to take disciplinary action.

Oral warning

An oral warning should not be used simply as a reprimand but should also stipulate adjustments in working performance, for example, that are required over a specified time period. The time period must be identified, along with the methods of assessment to be used.

Other disciplinary action

Information on any sanction imposed must be given in writing to the staff member. This must cover:

- the nature of the evidenced misconduct;
- the time period for improvement;
- how improvement will be assessed;
- how long the sanction will remain in place;
- the potential consequences of any further misconduct;
- the means by which any appeal should be made;
- the time limits allowed under the disciplinary procedure for an appeal to be heard.

Reasons for dismissal

Any staff member with one year's service has a right to request a written statement detailing reasons for dismissal. The manager by law must comply in writing within 14 days. The written information must comply with the oral reasons given for dismissal, as this statement may be used in any further proceedings by the staff member to support a case of constructive or unfair dismissal.

Right to appeal

A staff member who seeks to appeal against any disciplinary penalty must do so in writing within a set time period. A more senior manager will hear the appeal and that manager's decision is final.

Record keeping

Records of events must be written up and any disciplinary action confirmed in writing with the staff member. Staff disciplinary records must be stored in a secure and confidential place. These records must detail the nature of any offence and the disciplinary action taken, any appeal being lodged and the outcome of this, together with necessary assessment of performance if dismissal is not used.

Supervisory process

Disciplinary procedures are desirable as a dynamic means of improving staff performance. You can build into this an established supervisory system as a means of assistance to improve work output. This can be mutually negotiated over an already stated time span and followed through in a professional and structured manner.

CASE STUDY — Disciplinary procedures

You are a care manager in a 28-bed residential home for older persons. Increasingly, three members of staff demonstrate an inability to follow safe handling procedures. They prefer to lift rather than use the available aids for service user and staff health and safety.

- How might you handle this situation?
- How might you conduct your investigation?
- If there is to be any disciplinary action, what form might it take and how would you manage it?
- Make notes and role play this scenario with your peers using the disciplinary advice in this section for skills development purposes. Make use of observers for critical feedback of your performance.

Managing the grievance procedure

The grievance procedure enables individual staff members to raise concerns with their employer, irrespective of their status, relating to their working practices, their work environment or work-related relationships. Staff members may further seek to obtain appropriate redress. The grievance procedure becomes the necessary framework to facilitate this in a proactive and sensitive manner. When it is managed well it becomes another part of successful leadership. An example of a grievance policy statement is given in Appendix 1.10.

Staff members should feel able to raise their concerns with their employer

Procedures for practice

There are several simple rules that you should follow in grievance procedures.

- Advise all staff members to put their grievances either in writing or orally to their immediate manager. This could be a senior carer, a senior social worker, a staff nurse, a team leader or a care manager. Their manager should advise staff members of their rights to representation by a friend, relative or trade union representative. A written memo confirming the date of a meeting between a staff member and manager should be sent within a designated time period. The aim is to resolve the grievance within this period and the initial meeting should be at the earliest juncture for all concerned.
- If the initial meeting does not resolve the grievance, the staff member has the right to take a grievance to a more senior level of management. The same rights of representation and communication apply.
- If the second meeting fails to resolve the grievance, the staff member should be given the right to raise the grievance both in writing and in person at the highest management level. Within the mixed economy this may vary. Staff may seek a meeting with the director of the local authority social services department, the chief executive of the NHS Trust hospital or the managing director of a private or charitable organisation. Rights to representation apply, as does a defined time period when a written response to the staff member will be given. Most grievances are finally resolved at this stage.
- In accordance with the Data Protection Act 1998 and its rules on the confidential protection of records in a secure environment, the care manager must ensure an effective system of record keeping at every stage of the grievance procedure. It naturally must detail the original grievance and any actions taken; in addition, minutes of meetings can be given to the staff member, unless special considerations apply. Retention of records in a protected confidential environment is a priority.

Organisational limitations

Within the care service sector, some smaller private companies or charitable bodies from which care is purchased may not possess a comprehensive grievance procedure. It therefore becomes necessary to ensure good practice by recommending the services of a neutral third party to resolve disputes and maintain continuity of contracted care where necessary.

What if...?

If a member of your staff had a grievance, would he or she know how to respond and what steps to take within your existing procedures?

Preparing for a grievance interview

The preparation for a grievance interview is similar to that for a disciplinary interview (see Figure 1.5).

Figure 1.5 The process of preparing for a grievance interview

Content of the interview

Once again, there are some sensible rules and guidance that you can follow when carrying out a grievance interview. For example:

- Maintain the same standards as for a disciplinary interview.
- Be polite.
- Convey to the staff member that you are listening to the grievance.
- Assimilate the facts.
- Put things into context verbally for the benefit of yourself and others involved.
- Remember you need to understand the underlying reasons for the grievance being made.
- Allow the staff member to get rid of any anger, if appropriate.
- Clarify any areas you are unaware of or that require further explanation.
- Identify the organisation's procedural response.

- Resolve mutually where possible.
- Consider the next steps and ensure you both understand the consequences of any action taken.
- Reach agreement.
- Write up appropriate records and send them to the staff member; store copies confidentially.

Outcomes of grievance procedures

Careful management of both the grievance procedure and interview is critical. The aim should be to resolve the contested issue at the earliest juncture. The outcome for staff, service users and the organisation's reputation as an employer are really self-explanatory.

STAFF

The presence and use of grievance procedures demonstrate to staff that the organisation can be responsive to their needs and adapt or change, as far as contractual procedure allows.

SERVICE USERS

The procedures maintain a continuity of confidence of service users and carers in their care, which after all they have purchased.

ORGANISATION

They reinforce principles of good employment practice both internally and externally. The procedures serve to maintain standards of work performance and so may stimulate both the flow of work and the necessary contracts, which in turn will ensure sufficient profitability for operational activity, irrespective of the area of care provision. Additionally, proactive organisations can demonstrate to team members that their care managers really do care about their collective welfare, which should represent the aspiration of effective management practices. Equally, standards of work performance should be recognised as not simply an economic exercise but the benchmark of best practice.

CASE STUDY — Statutory change

You are a care manager working with two inner-city child protection teams. With the introduction in March 2000 of the Framework for the Assessment of Children in Need and Their Families, new time scales for proactive intervention, to include referral, initial assessment and core assessments, became mandatory.

Despite these statutory obligations, a whole team makes a combined grievance that the new time scales are unworkable given existing case-loads, lack of staff and lack of resources for safe provision.

Using the above advice on conducting a grievance procedure, how might you employ it to facilitate the statutory change in working practices and still preserve the professional working relationships with your social workers and support staff?

Consider your responses carefully in line with statutory and contractual obligations.

Summary

You should now understand the importance of ensuring that your care setting updates its policies and that your teamwork can evidence best practice. Compliance with the Data Protection Act 1998 will restore and promote confidence in your work. A new culture of confidentiality must be established where your team must be inducted to understand their rights, responsibilities and how they can contribute to maintaining data security.

Health and safety becomes not only a statutory responsibility but also a duty of care which is shared between the employer and employee to both report and work together to minimise risks and achieve a safe working environment for all. Equal opportunities legalisation possesses the necessary interrelationship to promote equal access to work, training and team development. Clearly, it is the procedure itself that becomes the essential vehicle to promote equality within a generic care team, thus enabling best practice to occur.

Discipline and grievance need not be demonstrated as a punitive experience but rather a statutory requirement to ensure resident and staff safety, as well as maintaining the highest standards of contractual work performance. A prerequisite of leading and inspiring your team(s) is to ensure that the above policies and procedures are collectively understood, supervised and regularly appraised to ensure they achieve the desired outcome of best practice in every instance.

Check your knowledge

1. Does your care setting possess a data protection policy? Do you understand its requirements? Could you convince a National Social Care Commissioner that you can demonstrate legal compliance to avoid any criminal repercussions?

2. What areas of your practice are incompatible with this legislation? What steps might you take to improve data protection of staff, resident(s) or any other third-party information held on manual or electronic systems?

3. What does a Health and Safety Policy Statement mean?

4. Who is responsible for managing health and safety in your care setting and how is this undertaken?

5. What arrangements must you describe and outline within your policy statement?

6. What must your policy statement include?

7. How does the practice of equal opportunities operate within your care setting?

8. Having read the legislation, what omissions in relation to procedure that impact on employment, training and staff development need to be addressed and improved in your care setting?

9. What are your organisation's disciplinary policy and rules?

10. How might your organisation's disciplinary policy and rules need to be reviewed to comply with statute?

Appendix 1.1 Example of a data protection policy

Glebe House. Data protection policy

Introduction

The Data Protection Act 1998 requires Glebe House to ensure secure storage of the information it collects and uses, and not to disclose it to third parties unlawfully. To this end, Glebe House will follow the data protection principles to ensure that personal data are:

♦ accurate;
♦ not kept for any longer than necessary;
♦ kept secure;
♦ relevant and not excessive;
♦ fairly and lawfully processed;
♦ processed in line with individual rights;
♦ processed only for a limited purpose;
♦ not transferred to any other country unless adequate and equivalent levels of data protection exist.

The Data Protection Act 1998 makes a distinction between personal data, such as the subject's name, address and contact telephone number, and sensitive personal data, which would relate to section 2 of the Act (and additions). The latter are personal data relating to:

♦ racial or ethnic origin;
♦ political affiliation;
♦ membership of a trade union;
♦ health-related history, including mental health conditions;
♦ marital status;
♦ sexuality;
♦ tax code and National Insurance number;
♦ age;
♦ criminal history.

Under the Act, any processing of sensitive data is subject to stricter conditions. Glebe House requires written consent from any staff member to process such data.

Understand your rights under the Data Protection Act 1998

All staff have the right to see manual paper data and electronically stored data held on their behalf under the Act. All staff must know what information Glebe House holds about them and why it has to be processed. Additionally, all staff must understand how to gain access to their personal data and, where appropriate, how to have it corrected or erased. Staff must also be aware of some exceptions to this process where the confidentiality of a third party might be compromised.

The procedure for accessing your personal data

Any requests to access personal data must be referred to Mrs Johnson; she is the Caldicott guardian and as such is responsible for all data protection. Staff are requested to give 10 working days' notice for access to their information, and to indicate the nature of the personal data they believe to be held. An appointment will then be arranged to enable suitable access.

Responsibilities of staff to maintain data protection

Staff must recognise they have mutual responsibilities as data subjects and data users. All staff are responsible for:

♦ verifying that any information they provide to Glebe House that concerns their employment is accurate;
♦ informing Glebe House of any change required to the information held, such as change of emergency telephone contact numbers, change of address, next of kin;
♦ discussion and recording information provided by residents and their immediate carers and that they comply with the Data Protection Act;
♦ principles contained in this policy statement together with any advice given by the home's Caldicott guardian.

Responsibilities of staff to maintain data security

It must be recognised and understood by all staff at Glebe House that unauthorised disclosure of either resident or staff personal data could result in action being taken against the home under criminal law. Staff have a duty to be vigilant and maintain the integrity of data security within and outside the home at all times. Therefore all staff must ensure:

♦ that any personal information they hold is retained securely;
♦ there is no unauthorised access to personal data (staff's or residents');
♦ there is no unauthorised alterations to personal data;
♦ there is no unauthorised destruction of any personal data;
♦ there is no unintended loss of personal data;
♦ there is no unauthorised disclosure to a third party, orally or in writing, of personal data pertaining to staff or residents.

Appendix 1.2 Example of a health and safety policy

The policy below is a fictional example. The intention is to illustrate the principles and to serve as a guide to best practice – not to provide a template. This policy relates to a typical residential care home for older people.

Statement of intention

The policy of Cederfield Residential Care Home for Older People is to provide and maintain as reasonably practicable both safe and healthy working conditions for all its staff. This will also include all equipment, information, training, supervision and safe systems of operation. Responsibility is accepted for the health and safety of other people, namely residents and visitors who may by implication be affected by our caring activities. A copy of this policy will be given to all members of staff and made available for external inspection. Arrangements to implement the policy, together with allocated safety-related duties and means of monitoring, are included below. The policy will be updated as required by legislative change, changing resident needs and organisational activity. To ensure this, the owner, Dr Phillip Reed, will review the policy and its operation every year. A copy of the review will be made available to the National Social Care Commissioners for inspection purposes and inspectors from the Health and Safety Executive as required.

Signed: *Phillip Reed*   Date: 15/10/03

The management team responsible for carrying out the policy:

Name	Role	Signed	Date
Dr Phillip Reed	Owner	*Phillip Reed*	15/10/03
Mrs Helen Evans	Care manager	*Helen Evans*	15/10/03
Dorothy Lloyd	Senior care	*D. Lloyd*	15/10/03
Amarjit Kaur	Senior care	*A. Kaur*	15/10/03
Ranjit Singh	Senior care	*R. Singh*	15/10/03
Roy Davies	Senior care	*R. Davies*	15/10/03

The sole person responsible for health and safety at Cederfield is the owner, Dr Phillip Reed. However, for the everyday delivery of the policy, those named persons above share the responsibility for all health and safety matters. Additionally, all team members have a responsibility to themselves and to each other to maintain and achieve a safe working environment. When a health and safety issue manifests itself, team members are required to report the matter immediately to their line manager.

To assist the owner in implementing the establishment's policy for health and safety, the following roles have been delegated:

Role	Person responsible
Risk assessments	Helen Evans
Accident, investigation and reporting	Helen Evans
Health and safety training	Helen Evans
Appointed first-aiders	Amarjit Kaur
Organising fire drills	Roy Davies
Providing and maintaining first aid equipment	Amarjit Kaur
Purchasing	Helen Evans
Electrical inspections and routine testings	Ranjit Singh
Collation and maintaining records for COSHH	Dorothy Lloyd
Pressure systems	Roy Davies

Other identified specialist activities, to include monitoring the policy: D. Lloyd, A. Kaur, R. Davies, R. Singh, H. Evans.

Procedures/arrangements for health and safety at Cederfield

♦ *Risk assessment.* All work-related activities must be assessed for hazard or potential hazard and evaluated. This activity must also include new and expectant mothers. Any assessment which identifies a particular hazard must be recorded in writing. Strategies undertaken to control risks to health and safety must be listed. Responsibility for undertaking the assessments to follow must be given to a delegated person.

♦ *Accident investigation.* The delegated person will investigate all accidents or situations which might result in an accident. The investigation will be thorough and reported back in writing to the management team. All accidents must be reported by team members to their line manager using the establishment's accident report form, signed and dated. The line manager must report back all recorded accidents to the management team.

♦ *Health and safety training.* Health and safety training will be the responsibility of the delegated person. It will be structured, ongoing and developmental, to take into account current or new regulations. As part of the induction training for new entrants, the delegated person will ensure on a staff member's first day of commencement that:
  ◇ the establishment's health and safety policy is explained, and a copy of the document is given, together with opportunities to read it and ask questions;
  ◇ actions required of staff in the event of an accident are explained;
  ◇ actions required of staff in the event of a fire evacuation are explained;
  ◇ the staff member's duty and personal responsibility to follow the establishment's procedures at all times are reinforced, including the responsibility to report any health and safety concerns and communicate this with colleagues and the immediate line manager.

♦ *Fire safety.* In the event of a fire, any action taken must follow the written procedure. In summoning the fire services, always dial 999 and ask for the fire brigade. Always give the establishment's name, full address, post code, nature of emergency and leave your name as reporter. *Fire evacuation procedures.* Escape routes must be clearly marked on every corridor and all staircases must be kept clear of any obstructions that inhibit safe evacuation. Fire doors fitted across corridors and staircase landings must have automatic self-closing devices, so that on closure they restrict any spread of smoke and fire. All fire exit doors must remain closed and not be wedged open for convenience purposes.

♦ *Purchasing.* Only materials and equipment which can be safely used and that comply with Cederfield's requirements together with national regulations prescribed by law may be purchased. Before any purchase order is placed, a delegated person must undertake the necessary risk assessment to comply with this policy.

♦ *Electrical safety.* Only electrical equipment that is professionally serviced and maintained by approved contractors will be used at Cederfield. This will include all portable appliances (e.g. kettles, toasters, irons, heaters, electric blankets, and televisions). All appliances used on the premises must be annually checked, stamped and dated on the appliance by the approved contractor. Electrical leads and plugs must not be allowed to trail across floors; therefore both furniture and equipment is to be appropriately sited, to ensure safety at all times. All team members must be vigilant of any electrical damage and/or misuse and report this to their line manager for repair or replacement.

♦ *Other arrangements requiring a risk assessment.*
  ◇ manual handling operations (see Manual Handling Operations Regulations)
  ◇ use of chemicals or substances which may be hazardous to health (see COSHH)
  ◇ the use of protective clothing and equipment
  ◇ where a risk of potential violence to residents or staff becomes evident
  ◇ installation and use of new equipment
  ◇ new and expectant mothers

- *Smoking policy.* Smoking at Cederfield is in one designated area, the conservatory at the rear of the premises.

- *The reporting of health and safety concerns.* Any team member noticing a health and safety concern which they cannot safely address must inform their line manager for resolution purposes.

- *Unauthorised persons and children's welfare.* An unauthorised person is any person or visitor who enters any part of the building which they have no reason to access. A responsible adult must supervise all children visiting family members at all times.

- *Contractual work at Cederfield.* Before any work is undertaken at this establishment, a copy of the contractor's health and safety policy, including a method statement, will be obtained. Any repair, building or alteration that includes the installation of new equipment by external contractors needs to be carefully planned to ensure the safety of residents and staff at all times. A person from the management team will be delegated the task of essential coordination to minimise risks.

- *Office safety and security.* Care must be given to the layout and storage of items to minimise potential hazards. The handling and lifting of equipment must be minimised and undertaken only with designated safe equipment provided by the employer. Ensure easy reach of materials to avoid bending or falls in relation to items stored on shelves; storage must be kept at shoulder height. All information, that is records on staff or residents, whether on CD-ROM or manual files, is to be deemed as confidential and to be protected in secure cabinets, to comply with the duties and regulations imposed by the Data Protection Act 1998.

- *Consultation to maintain proactive health and safety.* Cederfield has its own safety committee, chaired by the care manager, Helen Evans, and meets once a month. Its composition is drawn from members of the management team, the elected team members and residents. Its primary task is to advise on the implementation of all matters relating to health and safety. Its work will include consideration of reported accidents, reports from external safety inspectors and those members of the management team with delegated health and safety roles. The primary outcome of this committee is to assist in the continuous development and improvement of safety rules and safe systems of work.

- *Monitoring the policy.* Monitoring the policy is the responsibility of the owner, Dr Phillip Reed, and those delegated members of staff with specialist roles. Formal monitoring of effectiveness will be undertaken by the owner, delegates and the safety committee. They will be guided by reports of accidents and dangerous incidents. Their findings will determine what alterations to the policy are required to minimise risks and preserve a safe workplace.

Appendix 1.3 Procedural exemplar: employment

Recruitment

♦ Advertise widely, and use local and informal networks.

♦ Ensure advertisements are written in languages which reflect the multicultural basis of the community you serve – do not rely solely on English.

♦ Ensure that all advertisements omit discriminatory jargon and language.

♦ The contents of a job advertisement must include a job title, job description, the organisation's purpose, salary, qualifications, experience required, location of post and organisation, special benefits and, most importantly, how and when to apply.

♦ Avoid wording that may favour a specific group or that discriminates against race, gender, age or disability.

♦ Ensure job descriptions and person specifications are accurate, up to date and relate to the post on offer.

♦ All applications must be administered in the same way – do not differentiate by gender, age, marital status and so on.

♦ Use a skilled and experienced selection panel.

♦ Ensure the questions for and the manner of each interview are the same.

♦ Ensure the questions asked are relevant to both the job description and person specification.

♦ Make sure you understand the interviewee's answers – seek clarification where necessary.

♦ Always give interviewees the opportunity to ask questions.

♦ Bring the interview to a close in a relaxed, professional manner.

♦ Ensure that once an appointment has been collectively agreed, the successful candidate is informed first orally and then in writing. When acceptance has been given, a written contract of employment legally termed under section 1 of the Employment Rights Act 1996 is provided.

♦ Provide exit interviews for unsuccessful candidates, for their professional developmental purposes.

♦ Ensure compliance with the Data Protection Act 1998 in relation to written statements made at interview by panel members.

♦ Ensure consistency and eliminate the possibility of any discrimination in the recording of candidates' statements.

♦ Always check references. These must verify the name of person, previous position held, time spent in employment, experience and any special skills, assessed performance levels, ability to work in a team, attendance, honesty and why the employer would recommend this person for this position. Do not rely on a verbal reference, as it can be subject to interpretation.

♦ Do not make an employment offer in advance of a reference request.

♦ Do not use the candidate's reference before the interview as a means of influencing panel members. This may introduce the risk of bias and discrimination.

♦ Police checks are mandatory for all newly employed staff – see Standard 29.6 of the Care Standards Act 2000.

Training

♦ Ensure the induction of new staff remains the starting point of proactive training.

♦ Use only mandatory TOPSS induction Standards 1–5 as the lead for your induction programme, as required by Standard 30 of the Care Standards Act 2000.

♦ Ensure that induction is delivered, assessed and evidenced within six weeks of commencement of employment. Each induction programme since 1 April 2002 will be assessed by the National Standards Commissioners as an outcome of the Care Standards Act 2000.

♦ Structure your induction programme to the needs of your organisation and link it to the contract of employment.

♦ Ensure your induction programme allows candidates to absorb new information gradually, and certainly avoid a vertical learning curve (see the induction checklist in Thomas *et al.*, 2003, pp. 267–71).

♦ Implement Foundation training as identified in the Care Standards Act 2000 (Standard 30.3) to NTO specifications.

♦ Link mandatory induction training to sector skills specifications as well as a continuous programme of internal training to reinforce staff understanding of the principles of care, safe working practices, the worker/professional role and the organisation itself.

♦ All staff must receive, as required under Standard 30.4, a minimum of three days' paid training per year, for developmental purposes.

♦ All staff should have a personal, individual training and development profile in order to facilitate an accurate assessment and evidence of progressional training.

♦ Introduce NVQ or in Scotland SVQ training for all staff, as required by Standard 28 of the Care Standards Act 2000.

♦ Use the NVQ/SVQ structure to ensure 50% of your staff are trained to level 2 or equivalent by 2005, as required by Standard 28.1 of the Care Standards Act 2000.

♦ Why not make 50% of trained staff to NVQ 2 a minimum figure? There are five levels within the NVQ structure to allow for progressional training. Make training a paid, contractual obligation as part of team member's professional development.

♦ Ensure that training is enjoyable, fun and constructive. Its results can be assessed both quantitatively and qualitatively in respect of work, service user satisfaction, elevated staff morale and reduced staff turnover.

♦ Training not only inspires innovative teamwork but it also becomes the catalyst that enables best practice to emerge as part of a collective effort.

Staff development

♦ Create a staff development policy to ensure proactive professional development for all team members, irrespective of occupational status.

♦ Ensure the policy underpins each team member's ongoing training profile.

♦ Ensure that all staff development is supervised in accordance with Standards 36.1–36.5 of the Care Standards Act 2000.

♦ Organise supervisory contracts, which are obligatory for all team members.

♦ The care standards are merely your benchmark for minimum standards. Staff development demands that supervision develops the professional practice of staff, is supportive and educational, and promotes accountability, responsibility and personal autonomy.

♦ All aspects of team members' performance should be appraised in a structured and achievable way. This can be linked to the original contract of employment.

♦ Appraisal should be linked to the development of the team member and organisational practice. It should be kept simple and realistic, measured, evaluated and where possible combined with motivational performance-related pay.

♦ Staff development must be related to continuous practice development to improve team members' and the whole team's performance, together with organisational output, in unison.

♦ Staff development must be accessible to all, organised, structured and recognised as the norm of best practice.

♦ It can be both formal and informal, supportive and instructive; however, it must address the individual team member's needs at every level and at all times.

♦ Staff development must prevent stagnation, hence it should be needs led with an outcome focused upon staff mobility and retention.

♦ Staff development must be subject to continuous supervision, monitoring and evaluation to ensure it achieves its desired outcomes.

Appendix 1.4 Example of a disciplinary policy

Discipline at Work (ACAS, 2000) gives this example of a disciplinary policy in its Appendix 3.

(1) Purpose and scope

This procedure is designed to help and encourage all employees achieve and maintain standards of conduct, attendance and job performance. The company rules (a copy of which is displayed in the office) and this procedure apply to all employees. The aim is to ensure consistent and fair treatment for all.

(2) Principles

(a) No disciplinary action will be taken against an employee until the case has been fully investigated.
(b) At every stage in the procedure the employee will be advised of the nature of the complaint against him or her and will be given the opportunity to state his or her case before any decision is made.
(c) At all stages the employee will have the right to be accompanied by a trade union representative or work colleague during the disciplinary interview.
(d) No employee will be dismissed for a first breach of discipline except in the case of gross misconduct when the penalty will be dismissal without notice or payment in lieu of notice.
(e) An employee will have the right to appeal against any disciplinary penalty imposed.
(f) The procedure may be implemented at any stage if the employee's alleged misconduct warrants such action.

(3) The procedure

Stage 1. First warning
Oral warning. If conduct or performance does not meet acceptable standards the worker will normally be given a formal oral warning. The individual will be advised of the reason for the warning and that it constitutes the first stage of a disciplinary procedure. A note of the oral warning will be kept but it will be spent after … months subject to satisfactory conduct performance.

Written warning. If the misconduct or poor performance is more serious the worker will receive a first formal written warning from their supervisor. This will give details of the complaint, the improvement or change in behaviour required, the time scale allowed for this and the right to appeal. A copy of this written warning will be kept by the supervisor but will be disregarded after … months subject to satisfactory improvement or change.

Stage 2. Final written warning
If the offence is serious, or there is a failure to improve during the currency of a prior warning, a **final written warning** may be given to the worker. This will give details of the complaint, the improvement required and the time scale. It will also warn that failure to improve may lead to action under stage 3 (dismissal or some other action short of dismissal), and will refer to the right of appeal. A copy of this written warning will be kept by the supervisor but will be disregarded for disciplinary purposes after … months subject to satisfactory conduct and performance.

Stage 3. Dismissal or other sanction
If there is still failure to improve the final step in the procedure may be dismissal or some other action short of dismissal such as demotion or disciplinary suspension or transfer (as allowed in the contract of employment). Dismissal decisions can be taken only by the appropriate senior manager, and the worker will be provided, as soon as reasonably practicable, with written reasons for dismissal, the date on which the employment will terminate, and the right of appeal. The decision to dismiss will be confirmed in writing.

If some sanction short of dismissal is imposed, the worker will receive details of the complaint, will be warned that dismissal could result if there is no satisfactory improvement and will be advised of the right of appeal. A copy of this written warning will be kept by the supervisor but will be disregarded for disciplinary purposes after … months subject to satisfactory conduct and performance.

(4) Gross misconduct

The following list provides examples of offences which are normally regarded as gross misconduct:

♦ theft, fraud, deliberate falsification of records;
♦ fighting, assault on another person;
♦ deliberate damage to company property;
♦ serious incapability through alcohol or being under the influence of illegal drugs;
♦ serious negligence which causes unacceptable loss, damage or injury;
♦ serious act of insubordination;
♦ unauthorised entry to comuputer records.

If an employee is accused of an act of gross misconduct, he or she may be suspended from work on full pay, normally for no more than five working days, while the company investigates the alleged offence. If, on completion of the investigation and the full disciplinary procedure, the company is satisfied that gross misconduct has occurred, the result will normally be summary dismissal without notice or payment in lieu of notice.

(5) Appeals

An employee who wishes to appeal against a disciplinary decision should inform … within two working days. The senior manager will hear all appeals and his or her decision is final. At the appeal any disciplinary penalty imposed will be reviewed but it cannot be increased.

Appendix 1.5 Example of a statement of disciplinary procedure

Broad View Care. Policy statement: disciplinary procedure

Introduction

It is the practice of Broad View Care to encourage good standards of quality, performance and conduct at all levels of the company.

The nature of the service provided by Broad View Care is such that the highest standards of conduct at work are expected at all times.

This procedure formulates arrangements which will ensure a suitable method of dealing with disciplinary matters.

The procedure is concerned with misconduct and gross misconduct. Incompetence and unsuitability will be treated in the same manner as misconduct.

General provisions

1 This procedure applies to all employees of Broad View Care.

2 Employees should be told of the complaint made against them and be given full opportunity to state their case before a decision is taken.

3 At any stage in this procedure employees have the right to be accompanied by a fellow employee of their choice.

4 Employees should not normally be dismissed for a first offence, other than for gross misconduct.

5 No disciplinary action should be taken against an employee before there has been a full investigation of the complaint.

6 Employees have a right of appeal against any stage of the procedure to the consultant for care, or, if he has been involved at any stage of the procedure, to the consultant for management. If employees exercise this right, they should put their appeal in writing, within a period of seven days, from the issue of disciplinary action.

7 The decision to dismiss an employee will rest only with the consultant for care and the consultant for management.

8 All cases of disciplinary action in accordance with this procedure will be recorded and placed in the official records held by Broad View Care.

Counselling

Where a member of staff is failing to meet the standards of work performance or conduct, their manager will normally counsel them on an informal basis. This will take the form of an interview and should make the member of staff aware of the standards required, and where these are not being met, and should attempt to determine if there are problems related to the work situation with which help can be given and/or if there is a need for any further training. Consideration should also be given to any personal problems where these are volunteered.

It should be made clear to the member of staff when formal counselling is to be undertaken and where necessary they should be made aware that the disciplinary procedure may be invoked where the required improvements in the standards of performance or conduct is not achieved.

Procedures to be followed in the case of misconduct

Examples of misconduct include bad time keeping, unreasonable or unexplained absence, lack of application, rudeness to residents/relatives/visitors, damage to property, unauthorised use of telephones, drinking of intoxicating liquor in the residential/nursing home or training unit, smoking in hazardous areas, failure to observe health and safety policy, unauthorised use of Broad View Care property, and any other breach of Broad View Care regulations.

Formal action will be taken as follows:

Stage 1

Minor breaches of discipline, misconduct, poor time keeping, etc., will result in an oral warning given by the manager. A note of this warning will be made in the employee's personal file. The employee will be advised that the warning constitutes the first formal stage of the disciplinary procedure.

Stage 2

Where there is a more serious case of misconduct or an employee fails to improve and maintain the improvement with regard to conduct or job performance, the following steps will be taken.

A disciplinary interview will be conducted by the manager and consultant for care.

The employee will be informed of the nature of the complaint/incident and will be invited to give an explanation of the matter.

If it is decided that disciplinary action should be taken, the employee will be told the decision and later sent a letter in confirmation.

The written confirmation will state the following:
◆ Details of the misconduct that has occasioned the warning.
◆ Details of the necessary action to remedy the situation and any period of review decided on.
◆ That any further misconduct will result in:
  ◇ dismissal with appropriate notice
    or
  ◇ a further disciplinary interview in the presence of the consultant for care and a confirmed final warning, which, if unheeded, will result in dismissal with appropriate notice.

Stage 3

A final decision to dismiss will be taken by the consultant for care when satisfied with the facts of the case, the appropriateness of mitigating circumstances and after further interviewing the employee concerned.

This decision will be confirmed in writing by the consultant for care.

If appropriate, the employee may – by written notice – be suspended on full pay for a short specified period in which time such an investigation shall be undertaken (during the period of suspension the employee will not be allowed on the Broad View Care's premises without the prior consent of the consultant for care or the manager, and subject to such conditions as may be imposed).

Procedure to be followed in the case of gross misconduct

An employee may be summarily dismissed if it is established, after investigation and hearing their version of the matter, that there has been an act of gross misconduct, major breach of duty or conduct that brings the home or Broad View Care into disrepute. In particular this includes:

◆ insubordination;
◆ serious breach of safety rules;
◆ theft;
◆ fraud;
◆ being under the influence of alcohol or drugs during working hours;
◆ flagrant failure to follow home procedures and regulations;
◆ disclosure of confidential information;
◆ deliberate damage of property;
◆ disorderly or indecent conduct, fighting on Broad View Care premises or threatening physical violence;
◆ acts of incitement or actual acts of discrimination on the grounds of sex, race, religion, colour or ethnic origin.

The employee may be suspended on full pay while the circumstances of any complaint are investigated.

Appendix 1.6 Example of a letter for suspension from work

Our ref:
Date:

IN STRICT CONFIDENCE

Employee's name
Employee's location
[or home address]

Dear

I write to confirm that pending an investigation into allegations concerning ... [insert] you have been suspended from duty on full pay with effect from ... [date].

During this period of suspension you should not attend your place of work nor any other of Broad View Care's premises unless instructed to do so by your manager, or director for care, nor should you contact any residents. However, you will be expected to make yourself available for any meeting which may be arranged as part of the investigation.

This suspension does not constitute formal action under the disciplinary procedure. However, I feel that your presence at work could be prejudicial to the investigations being undertaken.

You will be kept regularly informed of the outcome of the investigation and if the matter is required to proceed to a hearing under Broad View Care's disciplinary procedure, you will be give prior notice of the details and the right to be accompanied by a fellow employee of your choice.

I shall contact you again as soon as possible regarding the outcome of the investigation.

Yours sincerely

Appendix 1.7 Example of a letter giving notice of a disciplinary hearing

Our ref:

Date:

IN STRICT CONFIDENCE

Employee's name
Employee's location
[or home address]

Dear

With reference to our recent conversation, I am writing to confirm that you are required to attend a disciplinary hearing on … [date] at … [time] am/pm, which is to be held in … [place], in the presence of … [names].

At this hearing the question of disciplinary action against you may be considered, in accordance with Broad View Care's disciplinary procedure, in relation to the following incident/offence.

[Detail allegation/offence.]

The foregoing allegation(s) will, if substantiated, lead to formal disciplinary action being taken against you, which could include dismissal.

You are entitled, if you so wish, to be accompanied by a fellow member of staff of your choice.

Would you please confirm, in writing, that you will be able to attend the above hearing, including, if appropriate, the name of your colleague.

Yours sincerely

Appendix 1.8 Example of a written disciplinary warning

Our ref:

Date:

Employee's name
Employee's location
[or home address]

Dear

With reference to the disciplinary hearing which took place on … [date], I am writing to confirm my decision to issue you with a … [specify type] warning. The reason for reaching this decision is based upon

[Details for decision.]

I advise you that this written warning will be placed on your personal file.

[Include a paragraph on action agreed to help the employee to improve performance and to explain the consequences of no improvement.]

You have the right to appeal against this decision to … [insert name and status] as set out in Broad View Care's disciplinary procedure, and if you wish to exercise the right, your appeal should be lodged, in writing, to … within seven days.

Please acknowledge receipt of this letter.

Yours sincerely

Appendix 1.9 Example of a letter terminating employment

Our ref:
Date:

IN STRICT CONFIDENCE

Employee's name
Employee's location
[or home address]

Dear

I refer to the disciplinary hearing which took place on … [date], in the presence of … [names]. I am writing to confirm my decision to terminate your employment with Broad View Care. My decision was reached after taking the following into consideration:

[Specify details leading to the decision to terminate.]

After taking all these factors into consideration, due to the seriousness of the offence, I hereby give you notice to terminate your employment with Broad View Care, with immediate effect.

You have the right of appeal against this decision to … [name and status], as set out in Broad View Care's disciplinary procedure. If you wish to exercise this right, your appeal must be lodged, in writing, to the director for management, within seven working days of receipt of this letter.

Yours sincerely

Appendix 1.10 Example of a statement of grievance procedure

Broad View Care Limited. Policy statement: grievance procedure

Introduction

It is the practice of Broad View Care to encourage good communication between employees and their manager to ensure that questions and problems arising during the course of employment can be aired, and, where possible, resolved quickly and to the satisfaction of all concerned.

Employees should be given a fair hearing in relation to any grievance that they may wish to raise in connection with their employment. A grievance is any matter which is grounds for complaint that cannot be promptly and satisfactorily resolved by the manager concerned and involves an employee or group of employees and/or manager. A grievance within this procedure shall relate to any matter affecting the employer's terms and conditions of service, but shall not include matters relating to dismissal or other disciplinary action which are covered by Broad View Care's disciplinary procedure.

Any grievance should be investigated thoroughly and sensitively and be resolved quickly in order that nothing be allowed to prejudice the care provided to residents and service users.

Until all stages in this procedure have been exhausted the status quo must be maintained.

Stage 1
The grievance must first be discussed with the employee's immediate manager, who will record details of the grievance and after due consideration give a response as soon as possible, but generally within 48 hours of the matter being raised.

Stage 2
If the grievance is not answered to the employee's satisfaction, he or she may discuss the matter with the next senior manager, who will obtain the immediate manager's record of the grievance, will record any additional information and will reconsider the matter. A response will be made within at least 48 hours of the day the matter was referred to this stage of the procedure.

Stage 3
Should the employee still remain dissatisfied, he or she may request that the grievance be referred to the consultant for care, who will discuss the matter with the manager and will give further consideration to the problem. A decision will be given in writing within one week of the matter being referred to this stage of the procedure. This decision will be final, and there will be no right of appeal.

References and further reading

Section 1.1

FURTHER READING

Carey, P. (1998) *Blackstone's Guide to the Data Protection Act 1988*. London: Blackstones.

Cyert, R. and March, J. (1992) *Behavioural Theory of the Firm*. New Jersey: Prentice Hall.

Bosworth, S. and Kabay, M. (2002) *Computer Security Handbook*. Chichester: Wiley.

Flynn, D. J. (1992) *Information Systems Requirements: Determination and Analysis*. Maidenhead: McGraw-Hill.

Cudmore, L. (2002) *A Practical Guide to Data Protection*. London: ICSA Publishing.

Senn, J. A. (1989) *Analysis and Design of Information Systems*. Maidenhead: McGraw-Hill.

WEBSITES

Data Protection Act 1998
www.dataprotection.gov.uk

Section 1.2

FURTHER READING

First Aid at Work: The Health and Safety (First Aid) Regulations 1981. HMSO.

Safe Use of Work Equipment: Provision and Use of Work Equipment Regulations 1998. HMSO.

Safety Signs and Signals. HMSO, 1996.

Barrett, B. and Howells, R. (1997) *Occupational Health and Safety Law*, 3rd edition, Pitman.

Health & Safety Executive (1993) *Health and Safety in Residential Care Homes*, HMSO.

Health & Safety Executive (1992) *Manual Handling Regulations 1992. Guidance on Regulations* (L23), HMSO.

Health & Safety Executive (1997) *Approved Code of Practice and Guidance*. HMSO.

Health & Safety Executive (2000) *Successful Health and Safety Management*, 2nd edition, HMSO.

Parsloe, P. (1999) *Risk Assessment in Social Care and Social Work*. London: Jessica Kingsley Publishers.

WEBSITES

HSE statistics on RIDDOR
www.hse.gov.uk/statistics/pdf/riddor01.pdf
HSE information sheet on RIDDOR
www.hse.gov.uk/pubns/hsis1.pdf
COSHH e-learning website
www.pythia.co.uk/coshh.html

Section 1.3

REFERENCES

Thomas, A., Mason, L. and Ford, S. (2003) *Care Management in Practice*. Oxford: Heinemann.

FURTHER READING

Clements, P. and Spinks, T. (1996) *The Equal Opportunities Handbook: How to Deal with Everyday Issues of Unfairness*, 2nd edition. London: Kogan Page.

Collinson, D. L. (and others) (1990) *Managing to Discriminate*. London: Routledge.

Department for Education and Employment (1996) *Employing People with Disabilities: Sources of Information and Advice*, DfEE.

Department for Education and Employment (1996) *The Disability Discrimination Act and Your Rights*, DfEE.

Ethnic Minorities. Aspects of Britain. HMSO (1991).

Parekh Report (2000) *The Future of Multi-Ethnic Britain*. London: Profile.

Rubenstein, M. (2003) *Discrimination: A Guide to the Relevant Case Law on Sex, Race and Disability Discrimination and Equal Pay*. London: Butterworths Law.

Thompson, N. (2001) *Anti-discriminatory Practice*, 3rd edition. Basingstoke: Macmillan Education.

Worsley, R. (1996) *Age and Employment: Why Employers Should Think Again About Older Workers*, Age Concern.

WEBSITES

Which magazine
www.which.net

CHNTO Library
www.culturalheritage.org.uk

European Social Fund News
www.esf.gov.uk/goodpractice

Didac Limited (training and consultancy)
www.didac.co.uk

Community Council of Devon
www.devonrcc.org.uk

Health and Safety Click Limited
www.healthandsafetyclick.net

Jobsworth.com – online employment contracts and policies
www.jobsworth.com

Safety Learning – online health and safety training
www.safetylearning.co.uk

Section 1.4

REFERENCES

Armstrong, M. (1998) *Managing People*. London: Kogan Page.

Sargeant, M. (2003) *Employment Law*. Harlow: Longman.

FURTHER READING

Incomes Data Services (1998) *Unfair Dismissal*. London: Incomes Data Services.

Chandler, P. (2003) *An A–Z of Employment Law: A Complete Reference Source for Managers*. London: Kogan Page.

Cowling, A. and Mailor, C. (1998) *Managing Human Resources*. Oxford: Butterworth-Heinemann.

TRAINING VIDEO

Video Arts, *I'd Like a Word With You*.

This video is particularly useful to assist identifying poor disciplinary interviewing techniques. It also demonstrates good practice in promoting how an effective disciplinary interview might take place.

WEBSITES

ACAS

www.acas.org.uk

CHAPTER 2

Tools and techniques

2.1 Communication styles to influence decision making and provide effective feedback

In order to lead and inspire your team, it is important to consider the way in which you communicate with your staff. The communication styles you adopt will directly influence team-based decision making and indirectly any feedback given to team members. The content of any feedback must be focused on improving actual and future performance. The focus here is on three particular styles of communication:

● submissive;

● oppositional; and

● assertive.

It is important that you are able to differentiate between these and to adopt a consistent style in your practice. The involvement of team members in decision making is discussed, with the aim of empowering team member participation and reducing the potential incidence of interpersonal barriers, which might hamper constructive and meaningful communication. Additionally, a section is dedicated to showing how you can usefully engage in negotiating decision making by using the negotiatory, consultative, facilitative and single-authority approaches both to lead and to inspire your team to engage in realistic decision making. The final section focuses on how to recognise the diversity of team members' abilities, to ensure achievable, effective decision making and feedback as the norm of best practice.

Submissive, oppositional and assertive styles of communication

Generally speaking, it is accepted that there are three major styles of communication at your disposal to achieve best practice in enabling constructive decision making and providing effective feedback to team members. These are:

- the submissive style – this minimises feelings of self-worth and is not a constructive style to be role modelled (and it needs to be sensitively addressed if it is communicated by fellow team members);
- the oppositional style – this is likely to incur both anger and disrespect and to be avoided as a single or overt communication style;
- the assertive style – this is likely to enhance the self-esteem and the self-respect of all involved.

In order to explain how these different styles can be used in practice, a breakdown of each is given in Table 2.1.

Table 2.1 Comparison of communication styles

	The submissive style	*The oppositional style*	*The assertive style*
Recognised as	A non-communication style whereby you relinquish your rights before others. You bow down at the hint of authority or potential conflict. In other words, your low self-esteem and low self-worth do not enable you to challenge or assert.	You believe your own opinion, attitude and action are beyond reproach and criticism.	You stand up for your rights while recognising the sensitivities and respect due to others and you actively convey this within your communication style.
Outcomes for staff	Explained simply in terms such as 'I am a failure' or 'My feelings are unimportant in comparison with those of others'. This creates what is generally termed as the victim syndrome, which does not allow you to see yourself as an equal to others, but inferior.	An attitude of superiority exemplified by terms such as 'I matter but your feelings do not!'	Staff might interpret this communication style as 'I matter' and 'We collectively matter', and will perceive that they make a worthwhile and valued contribution to the organisation.
The spoken word	Appears as non-committal, even to the point of being apologetic.	Voice is clearly raised.	Firm but not aggressive.

	The submissive style	*The oppositional style*	*The assertive style*
Body language	Head pointing downwards to avert eye gaze, humbled positioning and slight forward lean of the trunk.	Tension in body posture; eye gaze can become fixed and hands can become clenched.	The posture adopted is relaxed and equates with the message of the spoken word.
Practice outcomes	Potential feelings of inferiority, low self-esteem and common disregard by others.	This style directly or indirectly violates the rights of others and disregards the feelings of other team members. Team members may feel displaced or similarly display behaviours of anger, fear and tension. Personal respect inadvertently declines.	Respect of others as well as respect from others.

The assertive style is the communication style likely to demonstrate best practice. All its components focus on self-respect and seek to convey respect to others in such a way that the importance of both parties is never minimised. Most people hold opinions and wish to express a point of view; however, in some situations the same people who vocalise opinions are weakened as a consequence. You need to find a means of seeking and learning each person's point of view. Recognition that the rights of others matter and the principle of equality within the communication framework are always preserved when the assertive style is used. As both a practice tool, it becomes the obvious style both to employ and to role model to other team members. In essence, it becomes the style to lead and inspire your team.

Submissive style

Assertive style

Oppositional style

Styles of communication

CASE STUDY — Assertive styles

Susan is a care worker in your team. She has just begun full-time work, having passed her assessed six-week induction period. However, she remains almost subdued in the team and displays very submissive behaviours when faced with more experienced colleagues. How will you teach her to become more assertive and win back her equal status within the team?

- How will you go about discussing with Susan how she feels? Explain the techniques you might employ.

- What types of listening skills might you adopt (i.e. attention only or attentive)? Differentiate and explain why.

- How might you teach Susan the skills of assertive behaviour?

- Explain the importance of a mentor strategy, whereby Susan would have a mentor with whom to practise with or even role model against.

- You ensure that she learns both the skills of speaking and non-verbal communication, to work in synchronicity. Why is this central to learned communication?

- What forums might you employ for evaluation of progress? Consider these carefully, as Susan's rights within the team require protection and should represent a priority of effective management.

The assertive communication style can support decision making and lends itself to effective feedback in several ways:

- It helps to build realistic relationships between team members.
- It dissolves interpersonal barriers, which can hamper communication styles (see below).
- It facilitates negotiation in the decision-making process.
- It leads to a valuing of staff diversity.

Building realistic relationships with team members is intrinsic to effective decision making. Creative interpersonal skills will help you to persuade, motivate, negotiate, support, resolve differences, articulate ideas, respect and value the diversity of team members' cultural base. These skills are central to team-based decision making. Recognising the core steps in decision making can be as much a part of relationship building as taking the actual decision if it is to be mutually owned and practised.

To demonstrate this, an exemplar of a learning pathway is given in Figure 2.1. Its purpose is to illustrate the interrelationship between relationship building and decision making and to identify the key stages.

Stage 1. Acknowledge the problem
Differentiate between what is the actual problem from the individual's perspective. Employ qualities of sensitivity, empathy, respect, genuineness and non-judgementalism. Employ skills of negotiation, listening and mediation.

Stage 2. Own the problem
Having defined the problem collectively, recognise that it belongs to you and no one else. Then accept the responsibility of addressing the problem as a team. Employ skills of critical analysis, self-assessment, openness and unconditional acceptance.

Stage 3. Information collection
Focus on different sources of evidence which may offer different or creative methods of resolution. Employ skills of acknowledging others' viewpoints, and demonstrating a willingness to adapt and use informal interactions to encourage mutual cooperation in problem resolution.

Stage 4. Weight up the alternatives
Always examine the alternatives against the validity of the information collected. Employ skills of objectivity and consensus management.

Stage 5. Take the decision collectively
Collectively own the problem. Do not dither – implement the agreed decision. Employ skills of decisiveness, democratic/supportive leadership styles and energised motivation to succeed.

Stage 6. Evaluate effectiveness
Collectively your team needs to make a judgment on how effective and realistic your decision has been. A priority rating scale or defined evidence collection from a variety of sources can determine success or failure. Employ skills of removing interpersonal barriers, willingness to accept criticism openly and learning from experience. Accept that not all decisions will be the right ones and that mistakes should not represent a failure – merely a new starting point. Motivation at this point is critical to the development of effective working relationships.

Figure 2.1 A learning pathway: the interrelationship between relationship building and decision making

Reflect on practice

Consider the existing ways that you and your team collectively arrive at decisions. Do you recognise an interrelationship between the decision itself and team-based relations? Is there room to build on and improve individual and team relationships? Discuss your thoughts with your staff.

Barriers to communication styles

First, you must identify the barriers which actually affect the day-to-day working relationships between individual team members. Once you have identified a barrier you must 'own' it. Then consider methods of barrier removal. In essence, interpersonal barriers affect even the most basic forms of communication within the professional relationship, for example even a request or an instruction can be obstructed. The resolution of such problems must be constructive, and individual rights and sensitivities must be respected.

What if...?

If, as a care manager, you were faced with a small group within your staff team who generally resisted team tabled motions for changes to working practices, how might you employ group pressure to reduce tension and interpersonal barriers, yet still preserve team unity for task achievement purposes?

Interpersonal conflict resolution

Resolving interpersonal team differences is no easy task. As manager, you must recognise the subjective nature of the individual behaviours which your team members will present and set them apart from each other. However, these differences need not be seen as an obstacle, rather an advantage, as they represent the very uniqueness of your team with respect to knowledge, skills, qualifications and specialisms. This diversity must be both nurtured and valued to enable all team members to realise their own abilities. Ideally, this process should not be competitive, but should promote equality, mutual trust, support and unity, to ensure the continued development of your team.

How is this undertaken?

You can question what areas of a person's interpersonal style are in some way dysfunctional. Break this down into components and then agree respective minimum standards or a threshold of acceptable practice. If the gap is breached, then the person's style becomes unacceptable; that member of staff may then require disciplinary action.

Another method of resolution is to try to put yourself in that person's reality. That reality would be neither perfect nor unique, but it will offer you an insight into individual behavioural mannerisms within the context of team dynamics. Once you understand some of these aspects you can then follow them up in supervision and explore the reasons or rationale for the problem behaviour. Self-control may have to be learned by that member of staff. Nevertheless, it should be accepted that one person's reality is as valid as your own. A compromise or no-win situation is likely to arise. Hence there is a need for constructive negotiation to resolve dysfunctional interpersonal communication.

CASE STUDY — Interpersonal barriers

You have been recently appointed team leader of an established care team which works within a private residential home and partly as community carers enabling service users to live independently in their own homes. One of your staff, Kashmir Singh, refuses to accept your leadership and continually acts outside the boundaries of acceptable team behaviour. How might you understand his viewpoint and tackle the situation without accusations being levelled against you of being racist, prejudicial and disturbing team unity?

- Will you discuss with Kashmir in an assertive yet open and friendly manner the reasons for his behaviour? How will you evidence this?

- Will you attempt to differentiate behaviours which fall into either acceptable or unacceptable practices?

- How could you attempt to encourage Kashmir to face up to the outcomes of his behaviour?

- Will you look at the possibility of interacting differently with Kashmir and begin to learn and accept his reality? If so, why and how?

- Will you change the manner of your communication style with Kashmir and take on board his feelings and needs? Why might you find this method more constructive?

Negotiating decisions

Negotiating decisions within the generic care service sector can be both politically and practically difficult where service users (both young and older) become the subject of mainstream decision making. Where the facts of a case are vague, and perhaps even the desired outcome is unknown, decision making involves risk. Nevertheless, negotiation is a central part of the care manager's role; it is a skill that is required in order to lead a team effectively. Negotiating decisions will involve proactive discussion with your staff team to identify what kinds of decisions they will accept or compromise on. The key is always to clarify, with the individual and the group, what areas of a potential problem can be negotiated. Then you can creatively assist your team, reach a compromise acceptable to all and, perhaps more importantly, reach a decision which is mutually owned.

The care manager, irrespective of discipline, can approach decision making in a variety of ways, according to need and the resources available. Four specific approaches can serve to guide this process:

- the negotiatory approach;
- the consultative approach;
- the facilitative approach;
- the single-authority approach.

These approaches, detailed below, offer you a choice of how to engage staff in decision making. Each approach is different and it is therefore important to select which is appropriate to a particular situation, without relying too much on any one. As an example, while the consultative approach is by far the most democratic, it may not be suitable in an emergency, where time and personnel are not available. Try to maintain an eclectic range of approaches which marry with your leadership style and which are acceptable to your staff. This is where your skills in negotiating decision making will be put to the test. However, the benefits of inspiring your team to reach collective and mutually owned decisions can produce best practice, which must remain your prime consideration at all times.

As care manager, you need to decide on the best approach to negotiating decisions

The negotiative approach

This approach is focused upon reconciling conflicting views or ideas and securing a compromise acceptable to the whole staff team. To pursue this approach you must identify the problem areas which will be the main subject of negotiation.

What if...?

As manager of a day centre for over 50 older people, you are referred a person with a long history of mental health problems. An approved social worker will assist in the management of the person while a community psychiatric nurse will monitor medication. What practical problems might you anticipate with this placement? How might you involve your staff within a multidisciplinary negotiation process to provide accommodation and meet essential needs?

The consultative approach

The consultative approach is by far the most democratic. It requires listening to the views of others. Your priority is to identify the key personnel who can contribute towards a realistic and binding decision.

> ## CASE STUDY — Community project
>
> You are a manager of a community project working with young adolescents who have a previous history of offending. The project is part of an urban regeneration scheme targeted at improving the environment, housing and employment opportunities within an exclusion zone. Although targets have been met, future employment opportunities remain at risk without inward investment. What community leaders – local councillors, Members of Parliament, local business people and interest groups – could you involve? How could you consult and coordinate their involvement to ensure you reach innovative decisions within a realistic time scale?

The facilitative approach

This is perhaps one of the most difficult styles to adopt and manage because the final decision is not your responsibility. As care manager, your responsibility is to assist the team, or others, to reach a collective decision.

What if...?

You are a newly appointed manager of a multidisciplinary children's resource centre. The centre has a residential wing for 15 adolescents, a secure unit for six adolescents, a school unit which serves 10 excluded pupils, a fostering and adoption unit, a community support team, a juvenile justice team and a family support unit. What kinds of meeting structure might you consider to bring staff together to enable collective decision making to take place? How might you facilitate proper consultation while ensuring that decisions can be taken by individual staff members without constant recourse to yourself?

The single-authority approach

With this approach, no consultation is involved. Decisions are made by the person with the vested interest, knowledge and skills, without recourse to others.

What if...?

As a family support worker, you advise one family to manage their weekly income support benefit carefully, and devise a budgetary support system for them to pay their bills and have a small surplus to spend on their children's needs. By what authority are you operating to control the monetary interests of this family? Does this intervention potentially reduce the family's autonomy? How might this approach be modified to include and involve the family in their own financial decision making?

The value of staff diversity and ensuring staff's opinions are promoted

You should value the diversity among your staff as this will benefit current and future decision making. It is imperative to recognise the fusion of background and culture that exists within a diverse staff team. As a group, your staff will be able to draw upon a variety of strengths, areas of expertise, experiences and styles both to identify potential problems proactively and to suggest solutions.

Valuing the diversity and strengths of your staff is a key skill for all care managers

Effective feedback

The feedback you give to maintain and improve performance must be:

- confidential – the feedback remains within the remit of the team, is not disclosed to others and is always given in a private environment;
- performance focused – the feedback focuses on team performance only and not on subjective personality traits;
- positive – feedback must be a constructive process that is sensitive to individual needs, irrespective whether the feedback is positive or negative;
- a joint process – feedback must be a two-way interaction, to ensure the viewpoints of individuals and teams are heard and clarified, in order to address the agreed outcome areas;
- involve solutions – feedback should be a joint process in which you differentiate between what has been achieved and what needs to be improved.

What if...?

If you wished to give positive feedback to one of your care teams in relation to their collective efforts to achieve NVQ 2 standards, in accordance with Standard 28.1 of the Care Standards Act 2000, how could you deliver this with a view to encourage the team to address the next level? Consider the joint approaches you would need to engage in to plot the solutions in order to achieve the desired result.

Reflect on practice

Try to remember the last time you praised a member of your team. Consider what you said and the manner in which this praise was delivered. Question whether your delivery achieved the desired result.

Your feedback to team members ought to be constructive, as this will encourage future work performance. Under no circumstances must the process remain static. In order to facilitate the more creative kinds of outcome-related development, your feedback should focus on actual performance:

- Identify events or behaviours which can positively reinforce what staff have done, so that they can learn from and be encouraged to perform against them – in other words, benchmark.
- Focus upon how performance can be changed or what could be done differently, in developing both personal and work-related objectives.
- Examine objectives set and work plans to identify limitations and gaps in performance and generate ideas to close those gaps.
- Engage in continuous practice development (CPD) (e.g. self-assessment), which promotes measurable outcomes, both current and developmental.

When giving feedback, try to appreciate the diversity of staff perspectives (see above). Feedback must be delivered in a private, professional and friendly manner; the meeting should be conducive to open discussion. Consider using the ground rules shown in Figure 2.2.

These ground rules are more likely to empower a team to discuss their strengths and weaknesses, to understand the value of collective improvement, to plot solutions and to set up an agreed action plan which focuses upon improving future performance. Feedback that is naturally supportive and that can be undertaken in a practical way is likely to engender the types of partnership that achieves mutually desired outcomes.

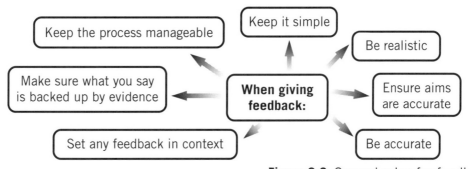

Figure 2.2 Ground rules for feedback

Reflect on practice

Does the manner of your feedback produce sufficient opportunities for your team to discuss their strengths and weaknesses in their performance and to engage in collective decision making?

CASE STUDY — Developmental team performance

Within the context of your team briefing structure, as manager you realise that the feedback you give to your team must seek continuously to improve future performance in the fast-track world of community assisted care.

- How might your feedback help the team to reflect on and learn from their actual work performance?

- How might your feedback assist your team to change their practice to improve performance?

- How might you modify your feedback to ensure that your team can evidence developmental change?

- How might your feedback help your team to identify their collective limitations, but with a view to resolve them through development and training?

- How might you structure your feedback to encourage your team to engage in more dynamic forms of self-assessment, to evidence continuous team development and improved practice?

2.2   Managing conflict

In order to lead and inspire your team and thereby achieve your goal of best practice, managing conflict becomes an unfortunate outcome of team building and team development. This section focuses upon common causes of conflict as well as the techniques to manage them. It differentiates between the types of conflict – namely intergroup, intrapersonal and interpersonal – you are likely to experience within your team. An examination is made of what positive outcomes can be achieved through proactive conflict management. Finally, there is an analysis of some apparent, perhaps short-term, 'solutions' that are to be avoided if team unity is to be preserved.

Conflict within team building is an unfortunate outcome of the process. If it is managed proactively there can be some useful learning strategies for actual and future practice. If left unresolved and unmanaged, conflict has the potential to be most destructive – it can tear out the heart and soul of a team, leaving a legacy of dysfunction. Moreover, best practice becomes unachievable.

Types of conflict

The first step in the management of conflict within your team is to distinguish its type (see Figure 2.3).

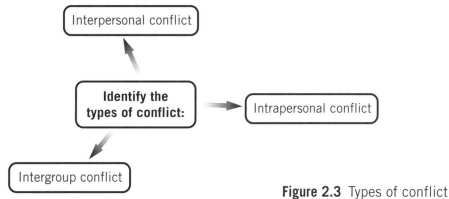

Figure 2.3 Types of conflict

What is intergroup conflict?

This type of conflict – between teams – is typically caused by a fight over resources. For example, two teams working within a large residential home for older people may fight over allocated overtime, or, in community social work practice, access teams for children may be in conflict with long-term work teams, over whose role it is to maintain a family unit and the associated costs if duplication of work arises.

What is intrapersonal conflict?

This is where conflict focuses on the individual and a disparity of loyalty you experience as a manager. For example, you discover that a long-serving and valued member of your team has been giving in false hourly work returns, and for some three months you have overpaid this person. You then experience anger and betrayal over misplaced loyalty.

What is interpersonal conflict?

This can occur when conflict arises between two or more people within a team. It could be between a bullying manager who scapegoats a particular member of staff, or it could be two teams of staff working back to back who seem to rival each other regarding everyday work practices.

Table 2.2 Strategies for resolving conflict

	Causes of conflict	*Management strategies for dealing with conflict*
Skills imbalance	If your team is deficient in relation to the variety of skills required to deliver care, individual team members may blame other team members or even management for this.	To resolve a situation of skill shortages, you will need to train existing staff, move around your skilled people, delegate, and employ new staff with the skills repertoire required, even if on a short-term contract, to ensure that training programmes for existing staff can succeed.

	Causes of conflict	Management strategies for dealing with conflict
Acceptance of low standards	If, as manager, you accept low performance standards as the norm, you may alienate those team members who seek to achieve to the highest level. Disenchantment is likely to result in both conflict between peers and a culture of demotivation (e.g. 'Why should I bother when my efforts are not recognised?)'.	Ideally, standards of care should be both qualitative and quantifiable. To operate in line with the Care Standards Act 2000, you must identify where standards fall below the minimum level. To close the gap, introduce standard setting for the whole team and monitor progress. Focus upon standards during supervision, introduce additional training, bring in mentoring roles as well as delegated roles where necessary and achievable. Most importantly, reward individual and team efforts where improvement can be reasonably quantified. Praise remains an essential developmental key to best practice.
Low team esteem	If individuals step outside their team role in the belief that their own skills set them apart from their peers, this can cause low team esteem, as well as deteriorating team performance.	As manager, it is your responsibility to uphold team unity and team spirit. If an individual or the team becomes dysfunctional, always ensure a team approach is taken to task achievement.
Lack of control	All teams require a parameter of rules to work within. If you relax those rules to a point where overall control becomes an issue, team members may accuse you of selective control or favouritism and this may become a source of team conflict.	Ensure that both the team and the individuals know what is expected of them. If control problems arise, they can be dealt with individually or with the team as a whole.
Practice change	Most people resent being forced to change their working practices or organisational policy – say, by legislative mandate. Unless teams can see the benefits of change, it is likely that denial will result in discontent or, at worst, refusal to change.	Teams do need to be consulted about change. Change can be driven internally – for example the changing needs of service users, new technology or new, flexible, family friendly work patterns – or externally – for example by legislation. In fact, change should become the norm of best practice. It is best dealt with by open discussion and consensus seeking about how the team can contribute and can change in the most constructive manner possible.

	Causes of conflict	Management strategies for dealing with conflict
Unclear leadership styles	If your team members are unclear about how or where they are being led, then their combined confusion might lead to conflict with the manager.	As leader of your team, irrespective of discipline or setting, you will be expected to adopt three roles: • a *guide* who offers a clear message to clarify a problem and most of all assist the team to achieve their roles and tasks; • a *controller* who is required to give specific instructions and is instrumental in guiding the team to achieve their tasks; • a *delegator* – while you must direct the overall task, ensure you delegate to each member of the team for task achievement purposes.
Role stress	Current legislation includes stress as a risk factor for working roles. Role stress can be caused by either overload or underload. Role overload can lead to members of staff feeling unable to cope. An inability to cope can often result in feelings of inadequacy which can result in conflict within the group. Stress may also result in serious illness, and even legal claims against employers who are accused of causing personal injury to their staff.	As care manager, you should show staff that you do actually care about stress and that you are prepared to do something about it. In order to reduce an individual team member's perceived stress, consult, reduce volunteered stress factors, and prioritise work tasks. This should also be done with the rest of your team, for reasons of equality. You should lead by example to show how to manage stress, and delegate responsibility, where necessary, but always with accompanying support and supervision. Stress relief is achievable if the symptoms are recognised as they manifest. Stress reduction can reduce underperformance.

Reflect on practice

Identify the current causes of conflict within your practice setting. List these and then prioritise them.

The positive outcomes of effective conflict management

Conflict within the work setting need not be considered entirely negative. If intergroup and interpersonal conflicts are resolved in a positive and inspiring manner, this can produce positive outcomes for team relationships and service delivery which benefit residents, staff and the organisation collectively. Initially, conflict can stimulate anxiety. However, it can create a creative and invigorating atmosphere that can inspire the way you lead your team and prevent stagnation and frustration.

By its nature, conflict can produce what is termed as exegesis – an outpouring of emotion. This need not be perceived as a problem. Frustration, if suppressed, can result in anger and then in conflict between individuals or teams. To inspire your team, establish a culture where the constructive release of emotion and feelings is a positive experience. In this way, team spirit and most importantly team unity are preserved.

Why not consider conflict as innovatory and dynamic? In other words, consider conflict as a natural outcome of teamwork that requires specific mechanisms to ensure its effective management. This requires proactive team consultation. It also demands an atmosphere of mutual trust, support and honesty, where individuals are free to question, constructively criticise practice and suggest pathways to improve service delivery. You can encourage your team to seek new solutions to existing problems. In this way conflict, either internal or external, can be managed and inspire best practice and, equally, be recognised as one outcome of organisational practice that is not negative!

Solutions to avoid

Some approaches to conflict may be superficially alluring, but will have negative effects on the team and service, especially in the longer term.

Avoidance, acceptance, appeasement

Conflict can arise over the simplest of issues, such as the hijacking of someone else's ideas and claiming credit. If you recognise a potential problem, try to avoid simply accepting the situation. Team problems do not simply disappear: they require resolution, by collective discussion and negotiation. Avoidance is a form of non-management that can demotivate team members and reduce trust and confidence in your management style. Appeasement implies taking the easy way out regardless of longer-term consequences and implications for all concerned. A *laissez-faire* approach, in which you avoid taking decisions to resolve conflict, can be perceived by your staff as a serious failure and flaw in your leadership style. This could have consequences such as lack of respect, demotivation or even high staff turnover.

The authoritative solution

It is important not to impose solutions on your team using your own authority as justification. Inspiring your team to resolve internal conflict demands that you address openly and honestly all areas of discontent. A variety of forums exist for this purpose – team meetings, team briefings, 'away days', or even very simple team-building activities. The adoption of a single solution based only on your authority, without treating the symptoms, is likely to have serious longer-term consequences.

CASE STUDY — Proactive conflict resolution

You have recently been appointed temporary manager of a medium-sized multidisciplinary community care company that has recently been bought out by a larger rival. The company offers a community care service to meet the different needs of some 600 home-based service users. Additionally, the company acts as an employment agency, which recruits staff to serve the needs of private residential homes, be it overnight, weekend or on short- and medium-term contracts. Residential care staff are required to meet NVQ level 2, as required by Standards 28.1 and 28.2 of the Care Standards Act 2000. A new arm of the company has recently begun to recruit trained nursing staff to meet the short-term needs of local NHS trust hospitals and primary health care teams. As an outcome of the takeover, staff tensions are high and there are concerns regarding job security, conditions of work and pay. The staff are demotivated. Given the temporary nature of your own employment contract, how might you motivate staff and resolve the concerns within the company?

- Will you attempt to recognise the intergroup, intrapersonal and interpersonal conflict in order to understand staff feelings and facilitate resolution?

- There are diverse causes of conflict within the company. List these in order of priority for resolution.

- What solutions to the conflict will you avoid? Give examples and potential consequences for practice of not avoiding these.

- What positive outcomes to conflict resolution might you pursue?

- What mechanisms might you put in place to reduce tension and create forums conducive to both discussion and problem resolution?

2.3 Maintaining confidentiality

Maintaining the confidentiality of the personal and sensitive information relating to both staff and service users is required by statute under the Data Protection Act 1998 and the Care Standards Act 2000 (Standards 17.1, 18.6 and 37.1–37.3) (see also Chapter 1). It is your duty therefore to create a culture of confidentiality. The benefits of this should be recognised and owned by the staff as a whole. The knowledge that personal information is secured and that access is limited to only authorised people and then only on a need-to-know basis can promote an atmosphere of trust, respect and confidence in your management of person-centred information. Part of your role will be to inspire team members to protect the confidence of their own and each other's personal information. The security that this knowledge creates can never be underestimated, particularly when fundamental trust and support are prerequisites of managed teamwork. The task is not that daunting and this section focuses on particular user friendly tools and their role in promoting best practice and enabling compliance with the law.

Maintaining the absolute confidentiality of all personal identifiable information might be reasonably perceived as impossible. No amount of legislation can protect confidentiality. Nonetheless, you have at your disposal a variety of tools and techniques to ensure compliance with the law.

Tools and techniques for maintaining confidentiality

Collectively, the tools and techniques shown can serve to create a culture of confidentiality for staff, service users and the organisation, but they will be of value only if they are put into practice in unison, managed and rigorously supervised. An additional safeguard is to include data protection into each staff member's contract of employment. Then any reported and supported misuse of information will immediately become a disciplinary offence.

Let us therefore examine these different tools and techniques that can be used within a team-based approach to achieve best practice.

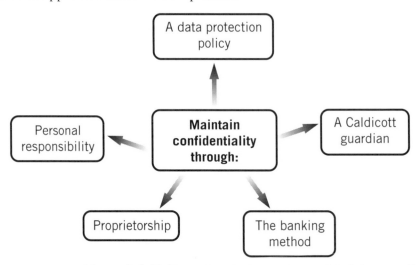

Figure 2.4 Tools and techniques for maintaining confidentiality

A data protection policy

In the first instance, a policy will simply be a written document. However, its importance lies in the fact that it stipulates what methods the organisation uses to ensure that information is retained in a secure, protected and confidential manner. Ensure that your data protection policy is simple to read and understand, accessible and can be transferred into actual practice. Only then can its real value be realised. All staff must understand that they are both data users and data subjects and as such must work to uphold the policy.

The policy should introduce the setting and then state its need both to collect and to use data, of course within the terms of the Data Protection Act 1998 (see the eight principles of the Act on page 3, Chapter 1, as well as the example of data protection policy in Appendix 1.1 of that chapter). It must make the distinction between personal data and sensitive data required under section 2 of the Act and further require written consent from staff members and residents to process this sensitive information.

A data protection policy can act as a teaching tool. It can help you to explain to staff and service users both their rights and how they can access their data. Equally, the policy must stress responsibilities, particularly of staff to maintain data protection and data security, and explain how this will be achieved, individually and collectively. However, for the policy to become a dynamic tool to promote best practice, it must be followed through using organisational mechanisms of team training, briefings, supervision and even appraisal. In this way, the policy avoids becoming a paper exercise and is evidenced as a practice tool with defined techniques for operational use.

For a new culture of confidentiality to be formed requires the participation of the whole team working together, subscribing and collectively owning the organisation's data protection policy. Frequent monitoring and evaluation of progress will minimise the risk of unauthorised disclosure and demonstrate compliance with all eight principles of the Data Protection Act 1998.

Reflect on practice

Re-read the eight principles of the Data Protection Act 1998 on page 3. How might you write your data protection policy to meet your specific practice needs and still comply with the law?

CASE STUDY — Data protection policy

You are a manager of a large assisted living complex owned by a charitable trust. The organisation provides accommodation for some 80 persons and employs 40 staff, both full time and part time, as well as an enthusiastic team of volunteers. You are aware of the implications and duties of the Data Protection Act 1998 but you still have no data protection policy to underpin your existing procedures. How do you move forward?

- Do you consider your existing procedures to receive, record, store and retrieve information on both staff and residents adequate? If so, explain why.

- How do you monitor the efficiency of these procedures?

- What documentary evidence might you share with your relevant Social Care Commissioner to demonstrate that your organisation complies with the Data Protection Act 1998, given the absence of a data protection policy?

A Caldicott guardian

A Caldicott guardian is sometimes referred to as a data protection officer. You may have one or more, depending on the size of the organisation. This person is responsible for protecting the confidentiality of all identifiable information (of both staff and service users) and for the implementation of your data protection policy. This is a dedicated post, held by a member of your senior staff team.

The role of the Caldicott guardian includes advising and supervising staff in relation to:

- how information is received, stored, accessed and retrieved;
- what information they record and how to record it;
- how to share information with their allocated service users;
- how to protect confidentiality at all times;
- the six Caldicott principles and their use (see page 5, Chapter 1).

What if...?

If you were considering appointing a Caldicott guardian, what skills and qualities would you look for? Jot down your thoughts.

CASE STUDY — The Caldicott guardian

You are the Caldicott guardian for a community village which offers a wide variety of accommodation for older persons. There are 120 full-time staff employed throughout the complex. The other agencies with which you interact include NHS trust hospitals, private and charitable health care companies, primary health care trusts, community-based district nurses, occupational therapists and private ophthalmic, chiropody and dental companies. Additionally, close contact is retained with local transport providers and leisure facilities. Information pertaining to residents, staff and external carers needs to be stored, recorded and transferred in a structured and legal manner. How could you do so with so many distracting variables and pitfalls?

- To what extent will all eight principles of the Data Protection Act 1998 be exercised? Consider the implications of your answer.

- What arrangements for data protection and data security might be set out in the data protection policy?

- How might you brief both your staff and residents on their rights and mutual responsibilities in relation to data protection?

- What different kinds of information system might you employ to hold data securely and confidentially?

- How will you ensure there is no unauthorised access to personal and sensitive information?

- How will you ensure no unauthorised alteration or destruction of data relating to staff or residents? What are your contingency plans to prevent or minimise this form of information abuse?

The banking method

The banking method is an organisational policy device for restricting access to the flow of information, which can be 'banked' in one restricted area (hence the term 'information bank'). Once information is received by email, fax, telephone, letter or memo, it is banked in one restricted area for confidential purposes. Only relevant and authorised people are allowed access and then only under the supervision of the Caldicott guardian, who would have to justify both access and use of this information and its immediate retrieval and transfer (and, indeed, who would be held accountable for its operational use to comply with the law).

This example of information security is one that might be adopted by other organisations to ensure the safe transfer of resident or staff identifiable information, as required by the Data Protection Act 1998.

CASE STUDY — Information security

You are a Caldicott guardian working for a voluntary community care organisation. Several of your existing service users have decided to choose other care providers, because you cannot meet their increasing dependency needs. Subsequently, requests are made to transfer their existing case files to other bodies. How do you proceed?

- Will you investigate the security of the new provider bodies' information systems before any transfer is made?

- Will you obtain written consent from your service users before any transfer is made?

- Will you contact any third party to ensure that its personal or sensitive data are not compromised?

- How will you satisfy yourself that any information transfer will not compromise the principles of the Data Protection Act 1998?

Proprietorship

A proprietor is someone who has been authorised to access, record, retrieve and hold information on service users he or she has been allocated to work with. Proprietors are selected (on the basis of experience, specialised skills, qualifications and honesty) and supervised by your Caldicott guardian. These crucial team members operationalise the process of protecting the confidentiality of all service users' identifiable information. They become the role models to inspire other staff as data users.

What if...?

If you, as Caldicott guardian, were to consider employing the proprietor role, what skills and qualities would you feel to be prerequisite?

CASE STUDY – Proprietorship

As Caldicott guardian, you have now selected and trained your proprietors to record, access, store and justifiably use resident identifiable information. In order to maintain compliance with the Data Protection Act 1998, you set up weekly supervisory sessions lasting 30 minutes to evaluate individual and team progress to establish your new culture of confidentiality.

- Will you ask them to list all the information, be it in manual or electronic from, for which they are responsible?
- Using their feedback, will you indicate how that information can be legally used?
- Will you identify with them what information they need to access and why?
- What measures to prevent unauthorised access will you seek to promote?
- Will you identify the limits of disclosure to service users' identifiable information?

Personal responsibility

All staff have a personal responsibility to maintain the confidentiality of all identifiable information on service users and staff. They must realise they are both data subjects and data users, and must use your data protection policy to prevent the disclosure of any information of a confidential nature.

Reflect on practice

Do your staff's job descriptions mention data protection? What third-party influence would you need to consider before changes could be instituted to job descriptions?

2.4 Analysing training requirements

Prioritisation of training needs and arranging training are a major part of the care manager's role. Training has a political dimension, in that equal opportunities legislation will apply and training may be demanded by government initiatives in both health and social care (training is therefore both desirable and, indeed, unavoidable).

In this section we explore the care manager's role in the staff training process. You will need to develop skills both in staff training and in recognising skills deficiencies on the part of your staff group. The outcome must be that staff possess the knowledge, skills and sensitivity required to respond to the different needs of service users at any given time. The section looks at how training can be undertaken at minimal cost, at what constitutes the components of a staff training plan and how that plan needs to be coordinated.

Having followed this process, the next step is to evaluate the success of your training plan and establish whether it has genuinely met the identified needs of service users, staff and the organisation. Realistically designed training plans justify their investment in terms of employee/team performance, motivation, self-confidence and improved standards of care. The satisfaction of service users is the best endorsement that managed training can achieve.

What is staff training?

Your principal resource is your staff. However, to harness this resource effectively requires training, for example to meet new legislation such as the Disability Discrimination Act 1995, the Carers Recognition (Goods and Services) Act 1995, the Human Rights Act 1998 and, of course, the Care Standards Act 2000, as well as new targets already being identified for 2007.

Following recruitment, selection and induction, ongoing training is the biggest single financial investment that you are likely to make. Therefore let us look at some definitions of what staff training is and how it might justify such a cost. According to Anderson (1995, p. 9):

> 'Training is a process to change employees' behaviour at work through the application of learning principles. This behavioural change usually has a focus on knowledge or information, skills or activities, and attitudes or belief and value systems.'

Alternatively, Bramley (1996, pp. 2–3) suggests that:

> 'Training involves learning, but it is rather more than that. Training implies learning to do something and when it is successful it results in things being done differently.... [It is a] process which is planned to facilitate learning so that people can become more effective in carrying out aspects of their work.'

Thus, staff training is located in the present. It represents a planned process of learning likely to incur certain behavioural changes which should have an outcome in activities being undertaken differently and more effectively.

As manager, you must realise that training becomes the inspirational vehicle with which to derive the behavioural changes you require of your staff. It is important that training produces specific and measurable changes. These are threefold:

- For staff, training should result in improved knowledge and skills, as well as the ability to undertake current and future professional roles.
- For service users, training should provide areas of improved service delivery that cater for individual choice and needs.
- For the organisation, a trained staff group should possess the required knowledge, skill, sensitivity and motivation to respond to different service users' needs and be able to comply with legislative changes, such as those introduced by the Care Standards Act 2000.

Your training plan should equip staff with the skills necessary to meet the individual needs of service users

In this way, training has a tangible benefit for everyone within the practice setting; it is a vital part of your management role in leading and inspiring team members. Staff training should be a learning process which is time efficient and usually directed towards the acquisition of specific knowledge and skills to fulfil current occupational roles and tasks.

There is often confusion between staff training, education and staff development. Education implies a longer-term process to prepare an employee to occupy a specialised role. For example, social work requires a minimum of three years' full-time study, and similar time commitments are required for degree-based nursing qualifications and accreditation. Staff development might be seen as an outcome of progressive staff training, but it is concerned more with the occupation of future roles rather than meeting current needs, which ordinarily staff training will address. The aim of staff training is to develop employees' skills and knowledge in order to improve their performance. Undeniably, care managers have a vested interest in this process to develop their services.

Table 2.3 presents examples of staff training and gives reasons for why the training would have been undertaken. As a practical exercise designed to develop your understanding of the need for staff training, study the examples given and then identify six or so types of training you have experienced and state why they were undertaken.

Table 2.3 Examples of the need for staff training

Type of training	Why undertaken?
Team-building exercises	To enable me to understand my own role, contribution and responsibility in developing effective team practices.
Unsafe handling techniques	To develop both my knowledge of safe and unsafe handling techniques with respect to assistance and movement of service users according to EU Directives (1992).
Review techniques	To develop my awareness of the variety of review techniques, how to apply them, and how to monitor and evaluate outcomes in relation to service users' needs.

How and where does staff training occur in practice?

Staff training can be as creative in style as the care manager chooses. Similarly, the care manager will choose the environment. Table 2.4 shows some examples of good practice.

Table 2.4 Examples of good practice in relation to how and where staff training occurs

Type of training	How it is undertaken
In-house training	Within the care setting. Most large organisations can provide training themselves, through their care managers in tandem with internal facilitators.
During supervision	In supervision it is important for the care manager to enable employees to acquire new knowledge and skills, or even to transfer the same to a new role (e.g. through promotion).
Team meetings	Weekly or fortnightly team meetings should accommodate a training slot. It need not be long but it does need to be specific to a particular area of need or an area the team has requested.
Mentoring/coaching	There should be a formal induction programme for new members of staff. A new member or inductee would be attached to a mentor or coach. An important part of this role is to assess the inductee's skills and knowledge. Where there is clearly a gap, specific training has to take place. The gap might concern a health and safety task, such as assistance and movement, the disposal of hazardous materials or catheter care. It might relate to an administrative task, such as daily, individual review of service users or taking telephone messages. All these examples would require specific and assessed training.
Peer training	A proactive care manager will recognise that certain experienced staff can take responsibility for training other members of staff. Apart from being a useful source of motivation, it serves to recognise and value the skills of individuals, and promotes trust and mutual support.
External training	It is not uncommon for care managers to utilise the resources of their local college of further education. The advantages are that most such training is time limited and can be tailored to meet exact needs. It also allows staff to network with other organisations and is usually cost efficient, particularly if the training attracts European Social Funding.
Internal training in an external environment	Care managers may choose a neutral training venue (e.g. a church hall or community centre) away from the care setting in which to conduct staff training. The value is that staff can learn away from the distractions of everyday work.
Competence-based training	In this formal work-based or 'on the job' training, a person's knowledge, skills, even experience gained over a period of time would be assessed by a qualified and accredited TDLB assessor on an NVQ (for Scottish boards an SVQ) range of 1–5. Most organisations will train to level 3, as levels 4 and 5 would be seen as qualifying and post-qualifying standards. The main range (1–3) focuses on expected employee standards in relation to a current role. The employee's competence would be assessed against specific performance criteria, in routine tasks such as making a bed to more complex ones, such as working in a team.

Type of training	How it is undertaken
Interactive computer-based training	This kind of training can be purchased off the shelf from a variety of software suppliers or even accessed online through private training operators. An employee would be expected to work through a computer package on the chosen area of training. One advantage of this type of training is that individuals can work at their own pace. The disadvantages are that participants must be computer literate, able to work autonomously and highly motivated, as support is not always immediately available. Despite the difficulties of this type of training, it is growing in popularity.
External trainers	External trainers can be brought in (for a fee) to cover areas of work where there is a lack of defined expertise. For example, a ROSPA-accredited trainer (see Chapter 1) could focus on techniques of assistance and moving service users according to the latest EU Directives. The advantages of this type of training largely relate to expertise and its time efficiency. A major disadvantage is that it can be very expensive if too much reliance is placed on it. You could network with other providers to train more staff within a programme and share costs between you.

Reflect on practice

Identify your preferred arrangements for training. Give reasons for your preferences.

Team meetings can provide a good opportunity for staff development

The components of a staff training plan

The pathway in Figure 2.5 serves as a guide to the components of a staff training plan.

Stage 1. Devise a training policy
Your own training policy, for the staff you are responsible for, must be aligned with the wider organisational training policy. This will ensure that all staff training is relevant. If no policy for training exists, write one and shape it around the training required. Keep the needs of service users the focus of the policy.

Stage 2. Identify the needs of training
Identify the aims of training. Keep them simple and achievable.

Stage 3. Set realistic objectives
Ensure that the objectives you set are realistic and relevant to both employees and service users.

Stage 4. Plan the training
Proactive planning ensures there is time to think the process through, to negotiate with others and to delegate roles. Consider the timescale, environment and cost of training. Take a macro view.

Stage 5. Identify and analyse need
Identify which specific needs to be met by training (see section below, 'How to assess the training needs of your staff'). Discuss and clarify with staff and service users and then prioritise those needs.

Stage 6. Formulate a training plan
Use information gathered in the needs assessment to formulate a training plan.

Stage 7. Implement training
The training plan should be implemented as soon as possible. Training may be delivered, for example, over one day or for one hour a week for six weeks. Once it has been decided that a training programme on a specific area is required, delay to its delivery is likely to diminish its appeal and its relevance.

Stage 8. Monitor and evaluate
Monitoring can begin even during training, via direct discussion with the team, in supervision or through the use of an anonymous questionnaire, to ensure that training is meeting its stated purpose. If not, make amendments. A final evaluation should be undertaken with all staff and with representation from service users. This evaluation might involve informal and formal discussion as well as written questionnaires. The priority must be to establish whether training has met its stated purpose or whether further training is needed. Each area needs to be evidenced to qualify value, relevance, learning and quality of service.

Figure 2.5 The components of a staff training plan

Reflect on the component cycle you have just read. In what areas might you need to encourage the participation of service users?

Coordinating a staff training plan

The staff training plan will need to be coordinated. It will be your responsibility:

- to plan the training and to involve others (including service users) in the planning stages;
- to ascribe or delegate roles for others to perform, to encourage ownership of the training plan;
- to communicate the plan to both staff and service users;
- to maintain the plan – to motivate staff to undertake and sustain training;
- to monitor training and to assess whether it has met its stated purpose.

How to assess the training needs of your staff

Staff training rests on the assumption that any staff group has identified areas of weakness/limitation where it can improve its service delivery. But how do you go about identifying training needs? There are a number of steps to take:

- Gather existing information pertaining to employee training and retraining.
- Explore and assess the organisation's or the team's training history.
- Observe your staff performing their roles.
- Compare your findings with others.
- Ask service users about the quality of their care and how it might be improved. (Consider carefully how they may like to be involved in this process.)
- Review all job descriptions. Differentiate between expected and actual performance based on your observation.
- Build up a staff profile, focusing on current level of skills and knowledge base.

The learning needs of your staff

In order to draw up a training plan that will meet your identified needs, you will have to have a good understanding of how adults learn. In order for adults to learn effectively, they need:

- to learn in an environment which is non-threatening and where anxiety levels are kept to a minimum;
- to know that their previous life or work experiences are valid, relevant and are transferable to different occupational roles;
- to recognise that their new learning is relevant to their current roles;
- to feel that their learning is being managed well and phased into achievable parts;
- to have time to reflect on what they have learned – frequent breaks, awareness-raising sessions, paraphrasing and so on.

Remember new learning is often difficult, so you must be prepared to offer support and encouragement to motivate the individual. In order for adults to learn effectively, you need:

- to eliminate any fear of failure;
- to provide opportunities for learning to be put to the test – promote activities, role-play, discussions and so on;
- to provide opportunities for self-assessment;
- to offer clear, constructive, critical feedback;
- to offer increasing opportunities, as appropriate for individuals, to plan their own learning and evaluate that learning in relation to practice.

Reflect on practice

Consider what other elements might influence adult learning. List them and explain their relevance to the learning process.

You will also have to consider the more specific styles of learning your staff present. Differentiating styles is intrinsic to drawing up a training plan that will ideally meet their collective needs.

On both sides of the Atlantic, since the mid-1970s a great deal of research has been focused upon how adults learn. Kolb (Kolb *et al.*, 1979; Kolb, 1984) and Mumford and Honey (1986) suggest that four learning styles categorise the learning process:

- *Activists*. These are individuals who enjoy the challenges and opportunities of working with change, or equally working with conflict in teams. They thrive on new experiences.
- *Reflectors*. These are individuals who will observe people, data and situations before taking a step forward. They will not be harassed into making a decision that is not first carefully thought through.
- *Theorists*. These are individuals who learn at their best when faced with a theoretical problem or issue. Their learning decreases if they fail to see any intrinsic value in the activity.
- *Pragmatists*. These are individuals who learn best when they can apply their learning to their current role and test out their assumptions. Their learning decreases if they are unable to apply in actual practice because of organisational apathy or where there is little relationship between what they learned and what they are required to do.

It is your responsibility to identify your employees' preferred learning styles. It is unlikely that all team members will prefer only one style. When drawing up a training plan, remember that an eclectic approach to learning seems more desirable.

If, as manager, you were seeking to determine the learning styles of your staff team, you could proceed as follows:

- Give the team written examples of the four learning styles.
- Ask them to identify their preferred style and explain why they prefer it.
- Then ask them how their view of training would be assisted or hindered by this style.

The collective responses will offer you an in-depth insight to how your staff prefer to learn and how training might be developed around those needs.

Considerations in the development of a staff training plan

Figure 2.6 serves to focus attention upon the key areas that require consideration before training begins.

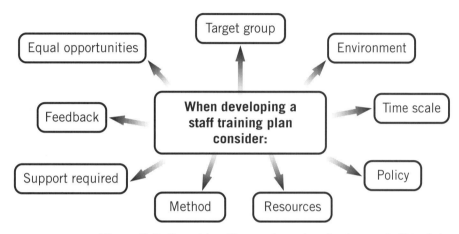

Figure 2.6 Considerations when developing a staff training plan

Training will naturally focus on staff needs, such as motivation or the implementation of new legislation. Nonetheless, it is important to retain a focus on service users throughout, and this may be a challenging task. It requires skill to ensure that all training relates to service users' needs and team needs in unison. Thus a demotivated team can be re-energised through team-building exercises with a view to improving care, as well as to sustain and achieve best practice. A team training plan, which is both realistic and meets identified needs, is relatively simple to develop, as the example below demonstrates.

Training plan to include:

- Introduce the new organisation and its principles during meetings with staff and service users.

- Demonstrate accurate empathy and take on board the views and concerns of both groups.

- Consider what new skills staff need to learn to protect and prevent unauthorised access to personal staff and service users' data.

- Identify changes required – to environment, security of information, systems (manual to electronic), access, records, retrieval – to comply with the requirements of the Data Protection Act 1998.

Aims

To develop a data protection policy to ensure that both staff and service users understand their rights under the Data Protection Act 1998. To ensure they understand issues and procedures regarding access to personal data. To ensure that staff understand their individual and collective responsibilities to maintain both data protection and data security in unison.

Objective

To induct staff and service users into a new culture of confidentiality.

Means

Team briefings and meetings with service users, to be held on a weekly basis. Both forums provide valuable opportunities to follow up training. If new areas or needs arise, consider additional training for this purpose.

Time requirement:

Two hours per week (one hour for each group) over 10 weeks.

Cost

Unit cost of 15 staff per week = £75 × 10 weeks = £750. Unit cost of meetings with service users covered by existing budgetary allowances.

Further points to consider

- Using the advice of the company solicitor for specified areas pertaining to unauthorised access and criminal ramifications.
- Follow-up briefing process within individual and group supervision of all staff.
- The same with service users during weekly review meetings.

Monitor

Weekly during and after each session.

Evaluate

At the end of the consultation period with both staff and service users collectively. Test out whether staff and service users understand both their rights and responsibilities. Ensure that the policy document underpins both the needs and the rights of service users and staff, and inspires confidence in both that policy and that best practice can protect personal and sensitive data. In this way the organisation moves forward in compliance with the law.

A team training plan to meet identified needs relating to data protection

Reflect on practice

Identify a specific training need within your practice setting. Then design a training plan to meet that need through negotiation with your staff and service users.

Questions to be asked when designing a staff training plan

- Do staff get paid when they engage in training?
- If they train in their own time, do they get paid overtime or are they given time in lieu, and how can their attendance be ensured?
- Particularly in generic residential establishments, who should receive training? Do you ask the cook or cleaner to general staff training days? Remember resident relationships are integral to the success of any staff training plan and in theory everyone has the right to train.
- How do you focus on skill requirements and roles to be developed?
- How do you establish your priorities?
- How do you maintain a genuine focus on service users in staff training, rather than token gestures?
- How are service users actually involved and what roles do they play? How are they supported?
- What arrangements do you make for staff training and how do you prioritise between external trainers/consultants or other trainers from within your organisation or other provider bodies?
- How do you network within the care service sector to access the specialist knowledge and skills available?

Evaluation of workplace training

Evaluation should remain an important feature of any training programme. The first step is to get accurate feedback from both employees and service users about the results of training. Further evaluation should examine whether:

- learning has actually taken place;
- there has been an effect upon the employees' behaviour;
- organisational goals have been met (or not met).

Evaluation will depend on the setting of clear objectives before, during and after training, as this will help to measure the impact upon the service users, employees and the organisation. The raising of standards is one such objective. Final endorsement will come from both service users and their external carers if standards improve. Evaluation must be continued in supervision, job appraisal or follow-up training sessions to ensure that training does genuinely meet identified needs.

Reflect on practice

Identify one piece of training you have recently undertaken. Ask yourself how it was evaluated and how might it have been better evaluated.

The benefits of training

The benefits of training should be threefold and recognisable to service users, the employee and the organisation.

Table 2.5 The benefits of training

Service users	The outcome of training must be that service delivery meets users' needs. It must also address the standard of care they both request and need (careful supervision should be used to ensure that the requirements of their individual care plans are met). Additionally, training should enable staff to have greater confidence in empowering service users to engage in decision making.
The employee	Training should have specific, measurable outcomes for team members. These must include improved levels of knowledge and skill. Opportunities to increase self-confidence as well as self-esteem raise levels of motivation, both individually and collectively, and so improve job satisfaction and personal ownership of work undertaken. Training should also be seen to increase opportunities for occupational mobility, which might indirectly increase staff retention.
The organisation	The benefits for the organisation of managed and inspirational training are manifold. It should produce staff with the required calibre of knowledge, skill and sensitivity to respond to the changing needs of service users. It will motivate staff, who will be determined to work towards higher standards of care. Additionally, training indirectly promotes the proactive use of supervision (in a variety of formats).

What if...?

If you were required to raise the profile of training to everyone within the practice setting, what potential benefits of training, to service users, employees and the organisation, could you give as examples? Give five for each.

2.5 Supporting individuals

It is important to use appropriate supportive methods that fit with individual team member's preferred learning styles be they: activists, reflectors, theorists, pragmatists. This involves the application of three methods of support, namely:

- individual support;
- small-group support;
- whole-team support.

The advantages and disadvantages of each method are considered below. In reality, their use as a tool and technique of best practice should dictate that too great a reliance on one would dissipate the learning of a significant proportion of the team. Hence the use of all three methods is likely to derive the required outcome.

Individual support

Individual support addresses the needs of both the reflective and theoretical learner. Both styles concur that the individual learns best when faced with a problem or issue and that before any decision is made they first need to think it through. Individual support offers time with the individual and facilitates the cognitive processes required by each style.

Strengths of this method

- It actively seeks the staff member's opinion.
- It offers mutual clarification.
- It enables open discussion.
- Participants engage in proactive problem solving.
- It identifies comprehension or a lack of it.

- It can build on previous learning.
- It can allay fears.
- It can reveal a skills gap.
- It can increase personal commitment to allocated work.

Potential weaknesses of this method

- It is time inefficient.
- Unit cost might be a problem if you cost your time.

- From an equal opportunities perspective it becomes inconvenient if you are required to clarify themes with all team members.

Small-group support

This form of support relates to the needs of those who are activists, pragmatists or theorists in their learning style. Application of learning, testing out of assumptions and the potential challenge of constructive conflict and problem resolution are an inherent part of this form of support, but it does meet very different needs in unison.

Strengths of this method

- A small group enables individuals to engage in risk taking in their discussion.
- Group solidarity can reinforce the need to convey and satisfy both objective and subjective feelings and thoughts, without inhibition.

- Group cohesiveness can confirm the interdependency of their existence and support of what they achieve collectively.
- The method is timely and cost efficient.

Potential weaknesses of this method

- A group method can sometimes result in the diffusion of individual responsibility for decisions reached.
- The group's needs may alienate an individual and inhibit valid contributions.

Reflect on practice

What methods of support exist in your practice setting that equate to the learning styles of your staff group. Give examples of what is practised.

Whole-team support

This method of support can be given to all learning styles (activists, theorists, pragmatists and reflectors) in unison. Whole-team support does require careful and sensitive management to ensure that all learning styles can be safely accommodated and challenged to ensure that they thrive on both their collective and unique experiences.

Strengths of this method

- It possesses an intrinsic cost-effectiveness, as all team members are present.
- The whole team receives and discusses the same information.
- Strengths can be identified from within the team and valued.
- The resources of the whole team can be applied, thus reducing the stress associated with a particular problem or issue.
- Less experienced or junior members of the team may feel less threatened and more energised by their counterparts.
- The fear factor can be minimised.
- Discussion can be as wide as the team chooses.
- Objectives may be individually focused or widened.

- Problems arising can be openly discussed, tested out and solutions proffered.
- Ideas can be built upon collectively.
- Non-verbal responses may be easier to ascertain within a managed collective environment. It also promotes the employment of flexible eye contact, which can ensure everyone is acknowledged.
- The clarity of team understanding, commitment and interdependency becomes a visible outcome.
- The group can set its own benchmarks for what can be achieved with existing team members, expertise, time scale and recourses.

Potential weaknesses of this method

- Open rebellion in numbers is possible.
- Quieter members of the staff team can hide behind the more vocal.
- Diffusion of responsibility is possible.

- Personalisation of issues rather than professionalisation can result.
- Equality of participation in a large group can be difficult to achieve.

Because of these potential weaknesses of whole-team meetings, it is essential for you to manage them well, for example by setting out ground rules before such meetings.

CASE STUDY — Day centre support

You are a manager of a day centre which caters for people with a wide range of physical disabilities. The age range of service users varies from 16 to over 60. Your different staff teams include support workers, teachers, physiotherapists, nursing staff, a counsellor as well as welfare rights advisers, who practise internally as well as in the wider community. Collectively your staff group possesses a diverse range of learning styles, which reflect the multidisciplinary nature of their work.

- What methods of support might be introduced to ensure that they equate with the individual team members' learning styles?

- Will you attempt to identify preferred individual learning styles (activists, reflectors, theorists and pragmatists). If so, why?

- Why will you consult team members about methods of support they prefer?

- How will you identify potential barriers to learning and consider strategies to overcome these?

- How will you evaluate progress in individuals' learning, using established forums of supervision and team briefings to ensure that these supportive mechanisms actually equate with team members' preferred learning styles. If so, how might best practice be shared?

2.6   Obstacles to team-based learning and strategies to overcome them

Team-based learning, if handled badly, can create team dysfunction and prevent team development and progression as a united group. Therefore it becomes important to identify potential obstacles proactively, and then to adopt a strategy to overcome them, in order to preserve team unity and inspire and promote best practice. This section focuses upon strategies that are realistic tools and techniques for practical application within the generic care service sector. Table 2.6 identifies obstacles that may arise and discusses a strategy to overcome each one.

Table 2.6 Obstacles to team-based learning and strategies to overcome them

Obstacle	Strategy to overcome obstacle
Anxiety	Minimise anxiety levels by promoting dignity and concern. This should be role modelled to the group, to develop a culture of individual and group value. This is exemplified by statements such as 'I matter' and 'the group matters'.
Assessment	Team learning does require frequent assessment of each individual's own learning and progress. Different formats can be used for this process, such as written assessment, or through discussion in pairs, or small or large groups. Equally important is honest feedback from the facilitator, which can be followed up in supervision.
Assimilated learning	New learning needs time to be assimilated. Useful means to facilitate assimilation are to paraphrase, summarise, remind and test out orally, in writing or by role modelling. People have different retention rates.
Atmosphere	Promote the notion of equality – all learners are equal, irrespective of occupational status, and everyone participating possesses the same right to learn. Rank does not rule!
Confrontational styles of facilitation	An inexperienced facilitator may present an abrupt or in extreme cases even an aggressive and manipulative style of teaching. This can create resentment and genuine feelings of being undermined. It may be necessary to encourage facilitators to adopt a more collaborative approach, in which all learners are not perceived as competitors but as equals, with a common sense of ownership and satisfaction in learning collectively without inhibition or fear.
Consultation	Consultation will empower team members to take part in the planning of their learning objectives and experiences. This can encourage ownership of any team training and individualises group learning.
Environment	It is important that the environment chosen is conducive to learning and affords maximum privacy and minimum interruption. Then at least new learning has a chance.
Formality	Formal teaching may be easier for some facilitators, as it will allow them to deliver a time-related event. However, formal teaching may be a pointless exercise if most participants simply 'switch off' because they are not engaged by the learning experience. This barrier can be reduced if you are able to persuade participants not to be inhibited by formality, although this may be difficult to achieve in practice. However, it may be possible to use formal delivery to ensure clarity of the subject matter, but then to engage the group in a more inclusive learning experience.
Group dynamics	All learning groups will have a set of natural processes or dynamics. It is important that these group processes do not become a barrier and create what is known as a 'frozen' group, stuck at a particular stage of development. Ideally, the facilitator will be aware of these variables, which can present verbally or non-verbally. It helps if the facilitator can deliver teaching and activities in a way which motivates staff to learn and that makes learning fun. In a mixed-ability group it becomes important to tailor activities and engage the individual within the wider group. Large group size can adversely affect group dynamics and cohesion. It is advisable to limit group size for active learning purposes to no more than 10.

Obstacle	Strategy to overcome obstacle
Instruction-based learning	Try to avoid over-reliance on instruction. Reduce this barrier by using the discovery method of learning. Individual and group members need to be able to develop skills in defining the nature and construct of problems themselves. An ability to ask the right questions in a manner conducive to a response can be the key to decision making and to finding the right answers.
Learning can be difficult	New learning can be difficult for many staff. Reduce this barrier by offering experiential knowledge, relevant theory, support and unconditional encouragement to all. After all, learning is a two-way process and mutual motivation can encourage group cohesiveness.
Managed learning	A team will present with diverse learning styles. An over-reliance (on the part of the facilitator or manager) on one style while ignoring others will extinguish essential stimuli. Hence an eclectic approach is by far the preferred method. Additionally, learning needs to broken down into manageable parts for comprehension purposes; perhaps this could be staged (i.e. tailored) at an individual level, thus preserving self-esteem and group unity.
Non-verbal communication	Non-verbal communication – or body language – offers clues to a participant's attitude, attention, morale and interest. For example, someone who leans back in a chair, folds arms and crosses legs is probably making a statement that he or she is bored. Conversely, a slight forward trunk lean can convey interest. Placing the finger on the nose or cheek may be interpreted as puzzlement or bewilderment. However, the reading of non-verbal communication is not an exact science, as it is governed by personal experiences that are subjective and highly individualistic, and the misinterpretation of non-verbal communication may represent a barrier to team-based learning.
Opportunities to practise different methods	Unless team members are empowered to experiment with their new learning – that is, to use new methods and approaches in their work – there is a danger of stagnation and of dynamic learning being extinguished. 'Return to learn' offers team members the opportunity to feed back on the advantages or disadvantages of methods or skills they have learnt. Discovery is often considered one of the more valuable tools in learning, so why make it a barrier?
Past experience	A team will be composed of individuals with different life experiences. It is important to stress the uniqueness of each individual and how rich in value each one is.
Present-centred learning	Ensure that team learning is focused on the present and addresses current needs and skills. Future-centred learning has a tendency to take individuals out of role, and relevancy can become both limited and short term.
Relevancy	Ensure that all new learning is relevant to all participants and certainly not just a few. All team members need to be aware of what they are to learn and why, and where this learning is leading.
Teaching of concepts	Teaching new concepts is far from easy and quite easily can overwhelm and engulf the group. Reduce this barrier by using concrete examples to make a specific link; emphasise a particular issue rather than general implications.
Timing	Allow sufficient time to cover the subject matter; allow opportunities for questions and answers, analysis of issues, reflection and role play (if required). It is best to aim to complete the exercise within a defined time span. Careful planning and objective setting ensure that the timing of activities is effective.

Reflect on practice

List the obstacles to your own learning. Explain why each is a barrier to learning.

CASE STUDY — Learning barriers

You are Jean's supervisor. A major focus of Jean's fortnightly supervision session has become direct teaching and learning. Jean has difficulties in translating recent legislation into practice. Instances recorded relate to data protection. How might this learning obstacle be overcome?

- How could you test her current understanding of the relevant legislation?

- How could you decide what teaching methods are appropriate to her learning style?

- What types of support might she need?

- What different kinds of reinforcement may be required to assist progression as learning and practice improve?

- What types of body language cues would you look for to confirm that learning is taking place?

2.7   Effective leadership styles and positive role modelling

The leadership style you choose to adopt when dealing with situations, staffing requirements or service users' changing needs represents an immensely powerful tool that can be successfully role modelled to team members. While it is appreciated that good leadership style cannot guarantee best practice, it can be inspirational.

This section focuses on three particular styles and two contemporary theories. You should compare and contrast them, and then choose which leadership style(s) would be best employed in your own practice setting to lead and inspire your team.

What is leadership?

Leadership styles refer to those intuitive skills and behaviours a care manager uses when occupying a leading role. It must be remembered that effective leadership evolves through experience of different work situations. A leadership style refers to a longer-term approach to assisting the team in service delivery.

There is more than one style of leadership and over-reliance on any particular one should be avoided. Your adoption of leadership styles must remain eclectic and able to be role modelled.

Before looking at the specific styles and theories, it may be helpful to outline the leadership skills required of the care manager. These are outlined in Figure 2.7.

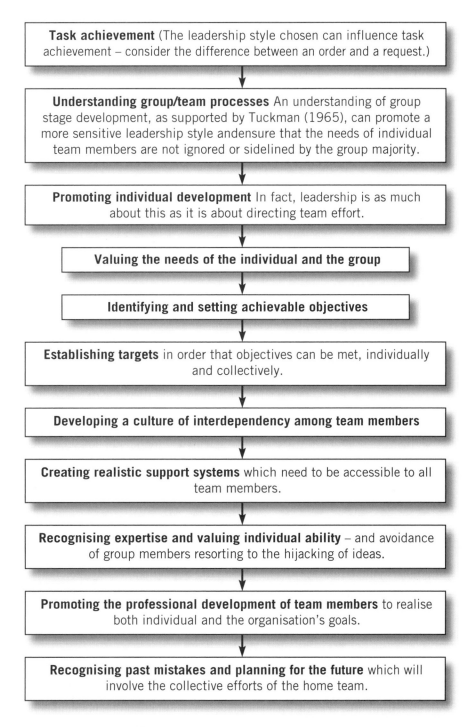

Figure 2.7 Leadership skills required by the care manager

Three leadership styles

Having made a case for effective leadership, it would seem pertinent to identify those forms of leadership style which can be used together in a sufficiently eclectic manner to be role modelled in actual practice (see Figure 2.8).

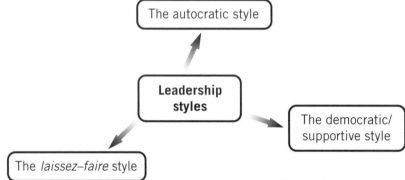

Figure 2.8 Three leadership styles

The autocratic style

When using this style, managers ensure that all decision making rests with them. Therefore they might expect compliance at all times and would use their authority to bestow merit or exact punishment. If, however, the style of leadership is too autocratic, it can create a climate of fear and lead to abuse of staff in its various forms.

The autocratic style of leadership means that all decision making rests with the manager

The democratic/supportive style

This is the complete opposite to the autocratic style. Here, leaders actively consult with their staff, they encourage participation and they give critical feedback on performance. Delegation is often seen as an outcome of this style, where team members are supervised to perform additional roles as a means of constructive professional development. This is a leadership style which is based on understanding the skills and abilities of team members, and so underpins a culture of trust and proactive support.

The *laissez-faire* style

This leadership style is commonly misconceived as an abdication of responsibility for decisions made, leaving staff lacking in direction. In its purist form it represents probably the most difficult both to develop and to sell to your staff team. In fact, far from leaving staff leaderless, this style promotes an autonomous and interdependent staff culture. There are provisos to its use: the style should be adopted only after team-building activities and only with experienced team members, to encourage them to work independently. Nevertheless, detached supervision is a basic requirement. The leader can delegate responsibility but not accountability for either task achievement or the delivery of care.

Role modelling leadership styles

The autocratic style is sufficiently eclectic to be role modelled, especially in emergency situations when direct instructions could even save lives. In a singular capacity this style is best left alone.

The democratic/supportive style of leadership is by far the most popular within the care service sector, as it role models the very best principles of effective management, support, trust, participation and professional development. Its consultative basis makes it a practical and not a utopian style.

The *laissez-faire* style does possess role-modelling capabilities in that it will free staff to make independent decisions without direct reliance upon management.

All three styles are constructive and useful; however, a reliance upon a single style reduces its influence. There will be occasions when an autocratic approach is demanded for immediate task achievement purposes. Equally, the democratic/supportive style will probably outweigh the former if staff are valued and requested out of respect to 'perform', rather than being ordered. Similarly, the *laissez-faire* style can encourage an autonomous and informed perspective.

As manager, you must be sufficiently eclectic in your management style to convey to your staff the most pertinent leadership style to their needs and tasks. Occasionally, styles may be combined, for example democratic/supportive with *laissez-faire*, where you might seek to role model consultation and participation with an outcome seen in confident and independent team practice.

What if...?

If, as manager, you were required to role model your preferred leadership style to your team members, what methods might you employ to assist both understanding and implementation of the particular style within the practice setting?

Other classifications of leadership style

As a point of good practice, it is constructive to compare the three outlined styles with some different examples of management/leadership styles. For example, Likert (1967) identified four styles of management:

- authoritative;
- benevolent;
- consultative;
- participative.

The authoritative approach involves placing little trust in staff and retaining total powers over decision making and control. The benevolent style is also similar to the autocratic style, in terms of placing little trust in team members and the fact that delegation is countered by strict controls on decision making. The consultative style is most akin to the democratic/supportive style: a manager might adopt this style when seeking the views of staff. The participative style also mirrors the democratic/supportive style, in that the manager would encourage trust, support, consultation and participation in all aspects of decision making relating to service delivery. Both styles value the principle of equality as a means of achieving mutually agreed goals.

In contrast, Fielder's (1967) contingency approach relates to three situational *dimensions*:

POSITIONAL POWER

This is akin to the autocratic style, where the manager derives power from the structure of the organisation and can demand compliance from the staff group.

TASK STRUCTURE

This moves the autocratic style one stage forward, for task achievement purposes. The manager identifies what tasks need to be undertaken and decides which individuals and teams are to be held responsible for them. The principle of unconditional compliance is again present.

LEADER–MEMBER RELATIONS

This dimension is more akin to the democratic/supportive style, where team members trust their manager out of respect and will display a willingness to engage in collective work after consultation.

Using Fielder's hypothesis it might be suggested that as situations (i.e. the needs of service users, or the internal or external environment) alter along these dimensions, a manager would need to adopt an eclectic style.

Both theories are related to the three styles of leadership outlined above. For example, contingency theory would support the idea that there is more than one form of leadership and no one style is always best. An eclectic approach is necessary for task achievement.

CASE STUDY — Eclectic leadership style

You are a care manager who has recently been given responsibility for a dysfunctional team which is unable to respond to change. You need both to get the team to respond and to role model an eclectic range of leadership styles to energise the group, to encourage consultation, participation, feedback and accountability.

- How will you consult with your team to explain the leadership styles you might intend to use and how will you take on board their feedback?

- In order to break up this visible frozen status, what types of maintenance skills might you employ to encourage a more sensitive leadership style?

- Having identified the group's preferred leadership styles how might you proceed to preserve group unity, responsibility and accountability for task achievement purposes?

- How might you role model an eclectic range of leadership styles to meet the changing needs of both individuals and the group?

2.8 Joint working arrangements

Joint working arrangements both within and between teams are increasingly becoming the norm within care settings. This is because they represent a realistic and manageable tool with which to achieve care planning objectives and subsequently promote best practice. This section focuses upon three levels of joint working arrangements – internal, external and multidisciplinary. Additionally, the potential sources of joint work and the need to engage in it are explored and supported with practice examples. To support the rationale that joint working arrangements might achieve agreed care planning objectives, a grid model has been designed to show how such a system can function in meeting the needs of service users.

Given the cost of providing care services by skilled personnel and the difficulties associated with recruitment and retention, joint working arrangements are a viable tool to ensure statutory service provision. It also promotes the value of realistic objective setting and the meeting of the different needs presented by service users and staff. In short, joint working arrangements are an achievable and inspirational method of working, which team members can be taught, to meet the specific and different needs of your service users, irrespective of the practice setting.

Levels of working arrangements

Joint working arrangements tend to occur at three different levels within the generic practice setting.

- internal;
- external;
- multidisciplinary.

Internal joint working arrangements

This is where a team will identify pairs of individuals to work together. For example, a pair of support workers within a small group home for people with a physical disability would share their expertise to run leisure activities chosen by the residents and to ensure that the activity meets the requested need. Activities might include water polo, ergonomic activities, and educational and outdoor pursuits. This is achieved by combining the joint knowledge and skills of two people.

Team members work together in an internal joint working arrangement

Reflect on practice

What internal arrangements for joint working exist in your practice setting? How could they be imaginatively improved to assist team members' development?

External joint working arrangements

This is where a team might identify one member within its ranks to work with an external expert. For example, a residential care worker adopting a key worker role might work with an external community support worker skilled in welfare and benefit rights. At the request of a resident of an older persons' home, they might research, identify and apply for benefits applicable to meeting the different dietary and medical needs of this resident, costed above what a local social services department might be willing to pay. Additional funds would greatly improve the quality of life of the resident. Increasingly, this type of joint work within the statutory and voluntary sector is becoming the norm to provide a top up to previously capped benefits.

Multidisciplinary joint working arrangements

This is where a carer in a residential facility might be required to work in unison with a community-based social worker, a district nurse working for a primary health care trust and an occupational therapist. For example, a resident within a local authority's residential home for older people requires a hoist to ensure safe and independent bathing arrangements. Because space in the bathroom is limited, a portable hoist is required, which is beyond the financial means of the resident. A tripartite assessment by the residential worker, a community social worker and an occupational therapist is required. A local community-based fieldwork manager, in conjunction with both the care and adaptations managers, would agree the purchase order.

This type of multidisciplinary assessment is common within the statutory, private, charitable and independent sectors, where funds are limited. Nevertheless, skills and costs can be shared to meet presenting needs within a fixed budget.

What if...?

If, as a care manager, you were presented with opportunities to engage in internal, external and multidisciplinary work, how might you go about this task?

Potential sources of joint work

Joint working arrangements, akin to other working practices, arise from particular sources. There are three common ones:

- budgetary restrictions;
- lack of skills/expertise;
- lack of personnel.

While all three sources in fact undermine the provision of care, they do demand joint working, which in turn may hold the key to meeting care planning objectives, as stated within the introductory comments to the Care Standards Act 2000.

Budgetary restrictions

Increasing costs and demands on cash flow require every private or public care setting to set a budget; this should be informed by proactive financial planning regarding input, throughputs and outputs. It represents the primary means by which the budgetary cycle can be quantified for profitability purposes. However, budgetary restrictions at any stage of the process reduce provision and both the capacity for service delivery and the quality of care.

For example, given the constant need to recruit staff within the care service sector, budgetary restrictions on advertising in the press reduce the ability to find the calibre of staff required. Outcomes within national and local NHS trust hospitals can be quantified by ward closures, cancelled routine surgery and increased waiting lists. This can be evidenced as a national but also a local problem.

Reflect on practice

Have you had to make cuts to the quantity or quality of services as a result of budgetary restrictions? If so, what steps did you take to minimise the effects of these?

Lack of skills/expertise

Care managers are required to maintain a balance of skills and expertise within their staff teams, to conform to safe working practices, as set out in Standards 38.1, 38.5 and 38.9 of the Care Standards Act 2000. With a shortfall of staff across the entire sector, this can become a precarious juggling act.

For example, most care settings (public, private, voluntary or independent) experience a problem in retaining basic-grade care, domestic/catering as well as senior staff without duplication of role. Balancing the needs to maintain an optimum number of staff and still deliver care, to set service standards which are externally monitored by the National Care Standards Commission, can become a regulatory nightmare.

The standards for older people (as stated within the Care Standards Act 2000) focus on the following:

- *Older people* – physical standards, as well as quality of life.
- *Fitness for purpose* – to ensure that care home managers, staff and premises are fit for their purpose.
- *Comprehensiveness* – to ensure life within a care home accommodates a range of services and facilities to meet the assessed needs of service users.

- *Meeting assessed needs* – the assessment and service user plan carried out in the care home should be based on the care management individual care plan.
- *Quality services* – in applying the Standards, regulators will seek evidence of a commitment to continuous improvement, quality services, support, accommodation and facilities which assure a quality of life and health for service users.
- *Quality workforce* – in applying the Standards, regulators will look for evidence that registered managers and staff achieve TOPSS requirements and comply with any code of practice published by the General Social Care Council.

On this basis, all providers are required to subscribe, as the Care Standards identify the minimum Standards below which no provider is expected to operate. To comply, care managers in all provisions of care for older people are expected to evidence their continuous regard for improved service delivery, quality, welfare, protection and maintenance of a quality of life that exceed the minimum criteria.

Lack of personnel

The lack of personnel to perform required roles within the care service sector remains a major problem. Its origins are both historical and contemporary, and include inadequate salary structures and, until recently, poor career opportunities. Care managers are expected to transform the sector from a vocational heritage into a profession. It remains the major challenge of the new millennium in both health and social care.

The lack of personnel in all parts of the health and care service sectors is a living testimony to the lack of regard politicians seem to have had for the caring professions. This has to be reversed. Perhaps it might be described as one of the major social changes of this new millennium. The Care Standards Act 2000 could become the benchmark for reform and measured change.

What if...?

If your budget increased, where would you begin to rebuild the personnel shortages in your practice setting to meet current and future needs? How could you measure the effectiveness of such a strategy?

Joint working and care planning grid system

It will be necessary to ensure that effective joint working arrangements achieve agreed care planning objectives. One way of doing so is the joint working and care planning grid system. An example is shown below.

Resident name:

John

Objectives set:

To be enabled to pursue individual social activities of own choice and increase personal autonomy.

Work plan to meet resident's needs:

John to identify social activities of own choosing and to prioritise these.

- Visit family once per week.
- Visit own parish church each Sunday morning.
- Shopping trip once per week.
- Trip to his local pub three times a week.

Joint working arrangements:

Please tick:

- Internal.
- External.
- Multidisciplinary.

Named key worker:

David.

Agreed time scale:

Two months.

Monitoring review:

Every two weeks.

Final evaluation:

Thanks to David's communication with the immediate family, John now visits his son once each week and daughter every fortnight. Family collects and returns.

John visits local RC Church for Sunday mass by pre-booked taxi.

Personal shopping is undertaken via unit's own minibus each Wednesday and in pre-booked taxi, as he requires.

John visits his favourite pub Monday, Thursday and Friday. David pre-books taxi and John confirms return.

An example of a joint working and care planning grid, completed for a resident

This grid system provides an excellent model to record care planning objectives, joint working arrangements, key worker role definition, time scale for agreed action, essential monitoring and evaluation of both process and intervention.

The grid system could be used for innumerable purposes to meet the different needs of service users, including:

- regular contractual respite care;
- vacations;
- making new friends;
- increased personal autonomy;
- permanent residence.

CASE STUDY — Joint working and care planning grid

Jane has been a permanent resident within your care home for three years. She remains active and self-caring and has expressed a desire to take an independent holiday to Alaska to celebrate her eightieth birthday.

- On what basis do you advise Jane on her planned holiday without inhibiting her basic human rights?

- What objectives will you need to set to meet Jane's expressed wishes?

- What might Jane's work plan consist of, taking into consideration her expressed needs?

- What kinds of joint working arrangements need to be considered to ensure that Jane's request and needs are met?

- How might Jane's work plan be evaluated and how might Jane be fully involved to realise her dream holiday?

- Reflecting on Jane's experience, how might the grid system meet the different social needs of other residents? Jot down your thoughts.

Summary

Having put your policies and procedures in place, it becomes your role, using the designated tools and techniques, to manage the process of leading and inspiring team members to engage in effective teamwork. You should have learnt about the interrelationship between different communication styles, their influence on essential decision making as well as the importance of feedback given to team members to improve actual and future performance. Additionally, in order to lead and inspire your team and thereby achieve your goal of best practice, it is important to recognise that managing conflict can become an unfortunate outcome of team building and team development. Therefore it becomes necessary to differentiate and address the different levels and causes, as well as solutions, of conflict to ensure that team unity is preserved.

Check your knowledge

1 Consider the three major communication styles, i.e. the submissive, the oppositional and assertive. Which one is more appropriate to employ in your care setting and why. Give examples.

2 What strategies do you have in place to manage and resolve inter-group conflict? Jot down your strategic rules.

3 What positive outcomes to conflict resolution might you pursue to preserve team unity?

4 Give examples of your existing procedures to receive, record, store, access and retrieve confidential information on staff and residents. Are they adequate to meet the statutory requirements of the Data Protection Act 1998?

5 How and where does staff training occur in your practice setting? State your preferred arrangement and why it is relevant to your personal learning style.

6 What current methods of support exist in your practice setting that equate to the learning styles of your staff group? Give examples of what is practised and encouraged.

7 Can you differentiate between the potential benefits and weaknesses of each method used?

8 Can you identify which obstacles represent a learning barrier which inhibit your personal learning?

9 How might you role model your preferred leadership style(s) to your team members? What methods might you employ to assist their understanding?

10 What benefits might you derive in your care environment from engaging in realistic joint work? Give examples.

References and further reading

Section 2.1

FURTHER READING

Evans, D. W. (1990) *People, Communication and Organisations*, 2nd edition. New Jersey: FT Prentice Hall.

Hadfield, G. (1999) *Beginners' Communication Games*. Harlow: Longman.

Lawler, T. (1989) *Design and Communication*. Harlow: Longman.

Melrose, W. (1995) GNVQ *Core Skills; Communication; Intermediate/Advanced*, 2nd edition, Pitman.

Noon, J. M. (1999) *Counselling and Helping Carers (Communication and Counselling in Health Care)*, British Psychological Society.

O'Sullivan, T. (1999) *Decision Making in Social Work*. Basingstoke: Macmillan.

Rakos, R. F. (1991) *Assertive Behaviour; Theory, Research and Training*, International Series on Communication Skills. London: Routledge.

WEBSITES

Article entitled 'Patterns of Communication Styles of Teachers in English 16 – 19 Education'
   www.triangle.co.uk/rpe/02-03/Harkin.pdf
Personal communication styles
   www.influencing-skills.co.uk
Questia Online Library
   www.questia.com/

Section 2.2

FURTHER READING

Department of Environment (1974) *The Health and Safety at Work Act*, HMSO.
Gardner, R. (1993) 'Preventing workplace violence: management considerations', *California Labor Letter*, August.
Home Office (1996) *British Crime Survey*, Home Office Research and Statistics Directorate.
Home Office (2000) *A New Era of Human Rights and Responsibilities*, Human Rights Task Force Secretariat.
NHS Executive (1999) *We Don't Have To Take This: NHS Executive Zero Tolerance Resource Pack*, Department of Health.
Trades Union Congress (1999) *Violent Times: TUC Report on Preventing Violence at Work*, TUC.

WEBSITES

NHS Zero Tolerance Zone
   www.nhs.uk/zerotolerance
Institute of Conflict Management
   www.conflictmanagement.org

Section 2.3

FURTHER READING

Carey, P. (1998) *Blackstone's Guide to the Data Protection Act 1988*. London: Blackstones.
Cordess, C. (2001) *Confidentiality and Mental Health*. London: Jessica Kingsley.
Parker, D. V. (1998) *Fighting Computer Crimes*. Chichester: Wiley.
Suddards, H. (2000) *Data Protection*, Chartered Institute of Personnel and Development.

WEBSITES

Leicestershire and Rutland Health Information
   www.leics-ha.org.uk
NHS Information Authority
   www.nhsia.nhs.uk
Florida Department of Health
   www.doh.state.fl.us

Section 2.4

REFERENCES

Anderson, A. H. (1995) *Successful Training Practice: A Manager's Guide to Personnel Development*, 2nd edition. Oxford: Blackwell.

Bramley, P. (1996) *Evaluating Training*, Cromwell Press.

Honey, P. and Mumford, A. (1986) *Using Your Learning Styles*, 2nd edition. Maidenhead: Peter Honey Publications

Kolb, D. A. (1983) *Experiential Learning: Experience as the Source of Learning and Development*. New Jersey: Prentice Hall.

Kolb, D. A., Rubin, I. M. and McIntyre, J. M. (1979) *Organizational Psychology: An Experimental Approach*. New Jersey: Prentice Hall.

FURTHER READING

Buckley, R. and Caple, J. (1995) *The Theory and Practice of Training*, 3rd edition. London: Kogan Page.

Hackett, P. (1997) *Introduction to Training*, Institute of Personnel Development.

Jones-Evans, C. (1997) *Perfect In-House Training: All You Need To Get It Right First Time*. London: Arrow Books.

Osborne, D. (1996) *Staff Training and Assessment*. London: Continuum International Publishing Group.

Section 2.5

FURTHER READING

Powell, S. (1999) *Returning To Study*. Buckingham: Open University Press.

Rogers, A. (1996) *Teaching Adults*, 2nd edition. Buckingham: Open University Press.

WEBSITES

Creative Learning Company
www.creativelearningcentre.com

Education for Adults
www.educationforadults.com

Resources Unlimited
www.resourcesunlimited.com

Section 2.6

REFERENCE

Tuckman, B. W. (1965) 'Developmental sequence in small groups', *Psychological Bulletin*, vol. 63, pp. 384–99.

FURTHER READING

Harvey, M. and Tisdall, C. (1992) *Vocational Qualifications in Care*. Birmingham: PEDAR Publications.

Howard, M. (1996) *How to Teach Adults*. Oxford: How To Books.

Knowles, M. (1990) *The Adult Learner – A Neglected Species*, 4th edition. Houston: Gulf Publishing.

Powell, S. (1999) *Returning to Study*. Buckingham: Open University Press.

Rogers, A. (1996) *Teaching Adults*, 2nd edition. Buckingham: Open University Press.

Whitfield, I. (1988) *Learning to Teach Practical Skills: A Self-instruction Guide*, 2nd edition. London: Kogan Page.

Section 2.7

REFERENCES

Fielder, F. E. (1967) *A Theory of Leadership Effectiveness*. Maidenhead: McGraw-Hill.

Likert, R. (1967) *Human Organization*. Maidenhead: McGraw-Hill.

FURTHER READING

Adair, J. (1979) *Action Centred Leadership*. Aldershot: Gower.

Adair, J. (1983) *Effective Leadership*. London: Pan Macmillan.

Adair, J. (2001) *Leadership Skills*. Chartered Institute of Personnel and Development.

King, S. (1994) 'What is the latest on leadership?', *Management Development Review*, vol. 6, pp. 7–9.

Lefton, R. and Buzzotta, V. (2003) *Leadership Through People Skills*. Maidenhead: McGraw-Hill.

Smith, E. P. (1982) *The Manager as a Leader*, Notes for Managers, Industrial Society.

Vroom, V. H. and Yetton, P. W. (1973) *Leadership and Decision-Making*, University of Pittsburgh Press.

WEBSITES

My Skills Profile
www.myskillsprofile.com

Section 2.8

FURTHER READING

Allan, K. (2001) *Communication Consultation*. Bristol: The Policy Press.

Copeland, J. R., Chen, R., Dewey, M. E., McCrachen, C. F., Gillmore, C., Larkin, B. and Wilson, K. C. (1999) Cases & Sub Cases from the MRC – ALPHA STUDY. 175 – 340 – 347.

Department of Health (2001) *National Service Framework for Older People*, Department of Health.

Hughes, B. (1995) *Older People & Community Care. Critical Theory & Practice*, Open University Press.

Lymbecy, M. (1988) 'Care management and professional autonomy', *British Journal of Social Work*, vol. 28, pp. 863–78.

WEBSITES

Northamptonshire Police: Western Area Working Partners
http://www.northants.police.uk/area/western/partners.htm

Achieving best practice

- 3.1 Use of supervision
- 3.2 Use of appraisal
- 3.3 Making presentations
- 3.4 Team briefings
- 3.5 Team building activities
- 3.6 Involvement and motivation of team members

3.1 Use of supervision

Supervision is one of the best ways of achieving good individual and team practice. This section concentrates on why supervision is such an important part of the care manager's repertoire of skills in managing both individual and collective practice. Supervision that is aimed at improving the occupational role, nurturing responsibility and accountability, and assisting in achieving organisational goals, irrespective of the work setting, is key to organisational success.

Best practice can be achieved through a well-managed supervisory programme. To enable you to do this, it is necessary to understand the term 'supervision' and the different processes it consists of. This section offers you the opportunity to explore your personal expectations of supervision as well as to differentiate between the types of supervision you could utilise. This should then enable you to make an informed judgement as to which might be the most suitable for your practice setting. Additionally, the differences between informal and formal supervision are discussed; these may be employed separately or in tandem. Best practice within the supervisory role is given much attention and it is emphasised that supervision must be seen as a process rather than as an event.

The key areas for achievement that you must address before, during and at the end of supervision are identified. It is anticipated that to achieve best practice with your team, you must evaluate performance at regular intervals. Recording the supervision process in both a manageable and accurate way is also covered, using appropriate examples from residential and fieldwork practice.

The rationale of this section is that well managed supervision should achieve best practice for the individual practitioner, the team and the organisation.

Supervision defined

The term 'supervision' has been used in the health and social care context for many years. So what exactly is meant by it? On the one hand, supervision suggests a process of social control and, on the other, it is seen as a means of developing professional, multidisciplinary practice. Perhaps the answer lies in the way in which supervision is actually used in the workplace.

There are many definitions of 'supervision' in operation at any one time, so only a few of the more useful ones are considered here – there are others that could be equally useful and appropriate. Betts (1993, pp. 3–4) describes the supervisor as any manager who controls non-managerial subordinates and is wholly accountable for their work.

Another definition comes from Drucker (1988, p. 243), who describes the role of supervisor as 'the connective tissues of an organisation and without them parts will not work together as a unit'. In contrast, Cusins (1994, pp. 10–12) states that supervision means:

> 'being able to look ahead and plan, look around to organise and co-ordinate the efforts of our people, look back regularly to monitor that we are doing what we planned to do, and if not to look into things and put them right by taking control and problem solving. Central to all of these, and essential for their effectiveness, is our ability to lead, to communicate and to learn'.

While the above definitions offer a degree of relevance, supervision could also be simply defined as an exercise in support, planning, connection, coordination, communication, training and accountability. It might be better to see supervision as the combination of all these activities in one general process.

Clearly, supervision must be two-way, focused, reflective, developmental and mutually accountable, aimed at improving knowledge of the occupational role and organisational responsibility. Only if supervision is seen as a supportive, two-way process can professional practice be individually and collectively nurtured to realise ability, performance and organisational goals, irrespective of the work setting; best practice can then be achieved.

Effective supervision

As suggested above, an effective supervisory system consists of an amalgamation of the following components:

- *Managing*. This is where the supervisor takes responsibility for ensuring mutual but accountable practice between herself- or himself and the supervisee. The outcome must be the shared planning, distribution, implementation and regular monitoring of work actually undertaken.
- *Accountability*. This ensures that negotiated tasks are performed by the supervisee to a high degree of quality. Accountability introduces the idea of standard setting and working towards measurable standards of service delivery.

- *Training.* A part of supervision is giving recognition to what knowledge and skills the supervisee possesses and giving them value. Identifying the new skills that are required to develop professional practice is also of importance and is a central part of the training and educational aspect of supervision.
- *Observation of practice.* Observation of the supervisee at work will give you an opportunity to give constructive feedback on the performance of specific roles.
- *Planning.* Effective supervision should seek to ensure that supervisees can plan their own work. With assistance, they should be able to set realistic targets for task achievement, which can be jointly monitored. Only consistent supervision can validate the process of planning work.
- *Organisational functions.* Supervision should seek to ensure that supervisees understand and can attain the functions and tasks required of them, within their own roles, as part of a team and also as part of the wider organisation. Supervision can also promote accountability on a dual basis.
- *Support.* Implicit to the supervisory task is the recognition that work in the caring sector can be stressful. Thus, a significant part of supervision must be to assist in stress reduction. You should aim to set realistic workloads and ensure that personal resources are employed effectively, thus enhancing the self-worth of the supervisee. In this way you can create a culture of coping.

Reflect on practice •

What are the components of the supervision you undertake? For each, say why it is included as part of the process.

Expectations of supervision

It is highly likely that managers and staff have different expectations of the supervisory process. For example, some staff could see the whole process as intrusive and threatening, while others could see it as supportive. The manager, on the other hand, could see the process as a mechanism for control or perhaps as a process for ensuring quality provision. You therefore need to ensure that there is a shared understanding of the purpose of supervision and not operate through a range of assumptions.

CASE STUDY — Ascertaining expectations of supervision

You are about to introduce a supervisor system into your care setting. In order to assess the expectations of staff with respect to the purpose, content, type and practice of supervision, you request them to complete the following questionnaire, after reading a sheet you have prepared explaining the types of supervision:

- What do you expect from supervision?

- What do you think supervision should involve?

- List the areas or aspects you think supervision should include.

- After reading the explanation of the types of supervision available, identify the one you would prefer. Say why you would prefer this model.

- What preparation would you want to see in place to support the supervisory process?

- How should your supervision be recorded?

At the end of this process you would have a clear picture of the staff's expectations. You would then need to resolve any problems you could foresee. Finally, you would share your information with the staff team.

Types of supervision

There are many types of supervision at your disposal. The key to success is to select the type or perhaps types that are most appropriate to organisational and individual needs.

Individual supervision

This is considered to be the oldest type of supervision and perhaps the one to be preferred, as it focuses on a one-to-one relationship.

ADVANTAGES

- It focuses exclusively upon individual development.
- It gives time to address areas of concern and their rectification within a formalised but mutually accountable meeting.
- It can be planned at mutually convenient times.

DISADVANTAGES

- It is costly in terms of time and money.
- If the discussion moves from the professional to the personal, it may be perceived as discriminatory or an abuse of power.
- If this type of supervision is not done regularly, then it may become merely a problem-solving exercise, at the expense of developmental work with the supervisee.

Tandem supervision

Here, two experienced workers supervise each other.

ADVANTAGES

- It develops a greater sense of responsibility among more experienced staff.

DISADVANTAGES

- Tandem supervision can be difficult for the care manager to monitor, which could result in an abdication of responsibility for the pair.
- It could also isolate the pair from the main framework of organisational supervision, leading to feelings of personal alienation or even team grievance.

Small-group supervision

A small group of staff (ideally no more than four to five) with similar needs and caseloads can work together to develop their practice. You should offer support and guidance, and help to manage group dynamics; you would also need to provide direction and to monitor progress.

ADVANTAGES

- This type of supervision may enhance interdependence within the group, as opposed to oppression.
- It might also facilitate more proactive monitoring and evaluation of both individual and collective progress.
- The supportive structures are dependent on collective accountability, which can be achievable given the demanding make-up of the group. If individuals do not work as a unit, the collective accountability collapses.

DISADVANTAGES

- Individual needs can be overlooked by group demand.
- Without consistent management, the group could dissolve into a support or even a pressure group.
- The care manager might be intimidated by working with a group of individuals.
- Issues of gender, race and power may enter the equation and require sensitive management to resolve and move forward.

Team supervision

This form of supervision is by far the most difficult and possibly the most contentious. This is when a whole team comes together to work on a specified task or tasks.

ADVANTAGES

- It is economical of time and therefore cost.
- It may provide a supportive and/or mentor function for new or less experienced team members.
- If managed well, it can serve to energise a flagging or dispirited team.

DISADVANTAGES

- It requires a very experienced care manager, who appreciates the power of group dynamics and the very ethos of a team being supervised.
- The overall management of such a large collective can be an intimidating task.
- There is scope for factionalisation or, at worst, scapegoating of team members.
- If tight control is not exercised, the team might engage in avoidance techniques or both individual and collective abdication of responsibility.

Reflect on practice

What type or types of supervision (individual, tandem, small-group, team) are used in your practice setting? Why are they used? List the advantages and disadvantages. Would other types of supervision be appropriate?

Styles of supervision

Broadly speaking, there are two styles of supervision that are available to the care manager. These might be briefly described as formal and informal.

The formal style

Formal supervision involves planning and usually takes place at regular, pre-set times, with both an agreed agenda and methods of reaching shared goals. Mutual accountability plays a major part in this process.

The informal style

Informal supervision will be unplanned and ad hoc. The agenda would therefore have to be agreed spontaneously. Some might think this is bad practice. However, what cannot be disputed is that, in actual practice, informal supervision with significant others or peers takes place constantly. Informal supervision can resolve problems or concerns as they arise, including those which are not properly dealt with in formal supervision. It is anticipated that, if combined with the former, it could make supervision a more dynamic vehicle of individual and collective development.

Reflect on practice

Which type of supervision, formal or informal, do you receive and why? How might you employ this type of supervision in your practice setting? How might the supervisory system be used to inspire your team?

Performing the supervisory role

Supervision has a process to follow, which will vary depending upon the type (individual, tandem, small-group or team) and style (formal or informal) chosen. Needless to say, there are certain obligations on both supervisor and supervisee to make it work. Appendix 3.1 sets out a checklist of what is required of the care manager before, during and after a supervisory session. It requires a re-evaluation of the statements at three monthly intervals to identify change and implement any remedial action.

Performing the supervisory role is not an easy task. It is one that requires training, experience and ideally observation of an experienced practitioner, as well as constructive feedback to aid personal development. If you view supervision as a process rather than an event, you can evaluate roles, decisions made and actions taken, as well as achievements. It can be a useful tool in developing self-worth for all involved and, of course, for leading and inspiring your teams.

Effective supervision requires training experience and constructive feedback

Recording supervision

You must ensure that records of supervision are brief and accurate, and that they are made at the time of the meeting. Records must represent an authentic summary of what occurred, when it occurred, any decisions made, by whom, and any actions to be taken. The record must be signed, dated and agreed by both parties. There is no reason why records of supervision cannot be produced on a shared basis, i.e. both parties take it in turns to record accurately what is discussed, agreed and to be actioned. This could serve to assist mutual ownership and encourage a sense of openness and genuineness about the whole process of supervision.

As far as is practicable, it is best to avoid establishing a 'paper culture'. One way of doing so is to use a pro forma for supervision records. An example of one is given below.

Staff Supervision Record

Name of staff member:

Aspects included:

-
-
-

Care manager's comments	Staff member's comments	Decision made	Action required	Time scale (date)

SIGNED (care manager):   DATE:

SIGNED (staff member):   DATE:

Example of a pro forma used to prepare staff supervision records

The record cannot be all-encompassing but it should detail the actual process of the session. Appendix 3.2 reproduces a record from the private residential sector. It represents an example of good practice.

Supervision in the public care sector tends to be more formal than that in the private care sector, especially if it is supported by a supervisory contract. For example, in child protection work it is now becoming the norm for fieldwork managers to be given guidance notes as well as a review form for each case file that the practitioner is working with. Then, during supervision, each case might be discussed in the light of criteria such as:

- time scales;
- statutory visiting/frequency;
- risk to child;
- their assessment and/or reassessment;
- filing of documentation, appropriately cross-referenced and up to date.

Any outstanding issues can be recorded, signed and kept within the case file. It becomes the supervisee's responsibility to maintain the case file, but the care manager is still accountable for managing the process and ensuring that standards of work are achieved. Furthermore, managers also have responsibility to ensure that records of work undertaken are accurate and maintained according to the procedural requirements of any given department. An example of such a supervisory case record is given in Appendix 3.3.

Reflect on practice ....

Do you have access to suitable supervisory recording systems? If not, design your own supervisory record, taking into account your organisational needs, work undertaken and the means by which you prefer content to be recorded. Discuss the record with your supervisees. Obtain input and draw up a pro forma, which can be mutually recorded and maintained. Through experience with it, refine it to meet your needs.

3.2 Use of appraisal

In order to sustain best team practice, one method that is often considered useful, if not essential, is appraisal. It is important at the outset to distinguish between appraisal and supervision. While there are similarities in structure, focus and developmental content, the fundamental difference lies in the role of appraisal in measuring team members' strengths and weaknesses through realistic target setting, to focus on key outcome areas of their role. The aim of appraisal is to improve the quality of care and organisational development, as well as to further the career aspirations of those undergoing appraisal.

This section begins by examining contrasting definitions of appraisal, and then goes on to explore methods of successful appraisal practice. Reasons for failure of the appraisal process are also discussed. The five-stage approach to appraisal is presented. This offers you a realistic and attainable means of introducing and undertaking appraisal in any care setting, and on a multidisciplinary level. Information on cost–benefit is included, as are techniques of good management.

The underlying rationale of this section is that effective staff appraisal can really make the difference to standards of care, to visible organisational change and to assisting team members' achievement and reward.

Staff appraisal defined

In the previous section we addressed the importance of effective supervision to professional development. Appraisal, too, can be used to identify strengths and weaknesses, with a view to ensuring that individual staff perform to the best of their creative potential as well as assisting with ongoing organisational development. How else might staff appraisal be described?

According to Mullins (1999, pp. 695–6):

> 'The process of management involves a continuous judgement on the behaviour and performance of staff. A formalised and systematic appraisal scheme will enable a regular assessment of the individual's performance, highlight potential, and identify training and developmental needs. Most importantly an effective appraisal scheme can improve the future performance of staff. The appraisal scheme can also form the basis of review of financial rewards and planned career progression.'

Furthermore, according to Pettes (1993, p. 238):

> 'Appraisal is essential for a number of reasons:
> - To give the employee a clear indication of progress and performance
> - To encourage ownership of roles and responsibilities
> - To assess the results of training
> - To obtain useful feedback information for the supervisor
> - To provide an accurate measure of progress for assessing merit rating relating to remuneration transfers, promotion and manpower planning.'

Both authors concur on the benefits to staff; however, they omit the potential benefits to either the resident base or the wider organisation in which people work.

Approaches to appraisal

Before you consider employing an appraisal scheme, it is necessary to be aware of two fundamental approaches that dictate both the required action and the performance. These are best described as informal and formal approaches to appraisal.

The informal approach

This can perhaps best be seen as representing an unstructured and ad hoc method of appraisal. It presumes that a systematic method is unnecessary, time-consuming and may even cause deterioration in the working relationships between management and staff.

It has a historical background in secondary and further education, where the focus would be on employee interests or aspirations and management preoccupation with evidencing staff development to access funding. In theory, the concept looks good on paper if the organisation is stable and staff are collectively working to shared goals. However, if informal appraisal prevents people from negotiating and setting their own targets, measuring and evidencing progress and being appropriately rewarded for a successful outcome, the following question would need to be asked. Is the informal approach a realistic appraisal situation or simply an annual review of what the employee might wish to attain, set against organisational targets? Furthermore, if the review process is simply a management signature of what the employee wishes without any form of interview, observation of practice or evidence of attainment, then the process of mutual accountability is lost and doubts are cast upon the realism of this form of appraisal.

A typical example of informal appraisal in further education is given in Appendix 3.4.

The formal approach

In contrast, formalised appraisal may be described as a structured, managed, monitored, measured and evaluated process. Here, you would be expected to sit down with a member of staff and engage in a face-to-face discussion. The focus would be on the role(s) within the current job description and the staff member must be empowered to identify specific areas or targets which might improve his or her future performance. In essence, individual performance and organisational goals are married through the precise nature of the objective setting. For this reason, a hybrid or five-stage approach model is set out below to enable you to make use of appraisal in both creative and achievable ways.

The five-stage approach to appraisal

This five-stage method is a useful tool in the manager's repertoire of skills. This approach to appraisal is systematic – that is, each stage must be worked through before you move on to the next. The five stages, which are discussed in detail under separate headings below, are shown in Figure 3.1.

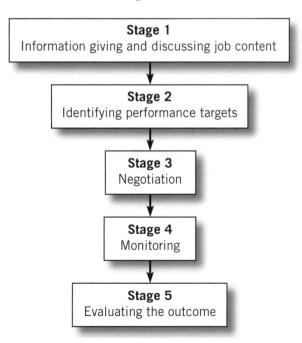

Figure 3.1 The five-stage approach to appraisal

Appendix 3.5 gives an example of a written procedure for staff appraisal using this five-stage approach. It shows how simple and realistic it can be in actual practice.

Stage 1. Information giving and discussing job content

The care manager and employee meet to discuss the existing job description. They must agree on the essential outcomes for the job to be conducted and thus define the employee's current duties. This provides an opportunity for the job description to be rewritten to equate with the post-holder's current duties.

The care manager must take care to ensure at this point that any changes to the job description are made following representation and endorsement with senior management and relevant trade union shop stewards, to safeguard the legitimacy of the process. Equally, the language used in the job description must accurately represent the current duties required of the role.

With these tasks achieved, the care manager can introduce the concept of appraisal, if this has not already been done.

Any aspects of the current role requiring improvement should then be raised and agreed with the staff member. In this process, ownership by staff takes priority. Break down the power barriers to ensure effective use of the appraisal system. Some members of staff are likely to require assistance and prompting. Discuss only those areas of role that could result in improved performance and service users' care. Remember that service users should be central to all discussions. It is vital that the final outcome area is chosen by the employee. Ideally, no more than one area should be considered at a time. Lengthy lists of improvements to outcome areas will be both unmanageable and unrealistic to fulfil.

Stage 2. Identifying performance targets

During this stage the employee is encouraged to set a specific target within the key outcome areas. No more than one area should be negotiated at any one time. The focus should be upon improvement in order to meet organisational circumstances, the needs of service users and the staff member's career aspirations. The target selected must be negotiated with the employee, who should be empowered to take the initiative in choosing an area likely to incur the most constructive change within an identified time period, say three months.

Bear in mind these key words when target setting:

- Specific.
- Realistic.
- Manageable.
- Mutually negotiated.
- Time-bound.
- Attainable.
- Balance of power (avoid using power to enforce actions).

Clearly, the choice of the performance target will depend on how informed the employee is about the scheme and how motivated he or she may be to see it through. Much depends upon the training and experience of the appraising manager, and knowledge of the competence levels of the employee is essential in identifying a realistic, attainable target.

There is a need to be realistic, particularly in relation to time constraints. Best practice would indicate a period of no more than three months, although this could be modified if organisational or individual needs change.

Stage 3. Negotiation

Stage 3 is by far the most important part of the process. Success or failure will depend on the skills of the care manager, who should enable employees to set a realistic but attainable performance target within the negotiated time span. Issues of power, perception of personality and behaviour must be put aside to encourage a framework of mutual equality and respect in this process. The main danger here is that if employees feel they are being forced to address issues they cannot attain, or meet organisational needs at the expense of their individual input, then the whole scheme could fail. Key-words worth remembering here are as follows:

- Fairness.
- Equality.
- Active listening skills.
- Enabler.
- Effective communicator.

If individual employees can be empowered to make their decisions they are more likely to own the process, identify mistakes early and work to put them right.

Stage 4. Monitoring

Stage 4 represents the monitoring process: it is important to assess whether the set target is being attained. To keep the monitoring process simple and less time-consuming, it is wise to set checkpoints at regular intervals to measure progress. Key-words worth remembering here are as follows:

- Timely.
- Simplicity.
- Measurement.

Employees should be encouraged to keep a running record of how and when their target has been attained. If target attainment is not occurring, then the target setting needs to be modified. However, it is far better if such decisions are made by the employee, to encourage continued ownership. Sensitive guidance by the care manager is essential at this stage, in order to lead and inspire.

Stage 5. Evaluating the outcome

One of the secrets of successful evaluation is to have in place a process of monitoring planned and actual performance. In the final evaluation, the employee is appraised on ability to set a realistic target and meet it. However, the appraising care manager is still accountable for the appraisal process and must not be seen to abdicate responsibility for the meeting of what should be an attainable target.

Key-words the care manager might wish to remember for reasons of best practice are as follows:

- Constructive negotiation.
- Equality.
- Support.
- Guidance.
- Regular joint monitoring.

If a target is not met, then action must be taken. However, any judgements made in this respect must be based on evidence. Whatever policy the appraisal scheme is set to achieve, negative outcomes must be evaluated critically if the process is to have any legitimacy. In this connection, it is important to note that, as well as the employee, appraising care managers are judged on their performance during this process. Managers must therefore be trained in the appraisal process.

It is best practice for success to be appropriately rewarded and that this bestowing of merit, be it financial or otherwise, is done without delay.

While the evaluation will consider how the organisation has benefited and what further work might be undertaken in the future, the most important consideration is service users. Are they happy? Service users should be involved from the first interface to the conclusion of the appraisal process.

- Have their circumstances changed?
- What are their feelings?
- What of the views of external carers, family, friends and other workers?

Only an honest, comprehensive evaluation of the process will evidence its actual and potential value. Clearly, care managers facing appraisal situations for the first time require formal training in appraisal. However, even the most experienced appraising managers require the opportunity to consolidate, sharpen and develop their skills to meet different appraisal situations, such as a job transfer or promotion.

Why should staff appraisal be employed in the work setting?

Most companies, either statutory, trust, private or charitable, that genuinely promote successful appraisal schemes agree that they can assist in the following areas:

- They promote employee initiative and imagination, expressed through individual and team practice.
- They generate a desire for individual and organisational success and make this success highly visible.
- They motivate employees through personal ownership of organisational goals, which are kept realistic, through reward via payment by increment, discounted share purchase or any other negotiated form.

- They can create a sense of mutual responsibility to peers as well as the organisation in a competitive marketplace. They generally foster the recognition that the needs of people at work matter.

Additionally, schools of thought within occupational psychology increasingly promote the view that employees want:

- to be given active input in relation to organisational change;
- their views to matter and make a difference;
- constructive and equal support;
- accurate feedback regarding their performance;
- to achieve their own goals, to identify their own training needs and to be given support to realise their potential within the parameters of organisational need and output;
- to see their individual efforts succeed and to be appropriately recognised;
- to be rewarded fairly for those efforts.

Many staff aspirations appear simple but if supported could offer personal fulfilment, increased satisfaction (on the part of service users as well as staff) and real organisational development.

Examples of appraisal in practice

EXAMPLE 1
A general practitioner's customer support worker seeks to reduce the number of unattended appointments. This could increase the number of patients seen more promptly.

EXAMPLE 2
A senior care worker in a residential nursing home for people with long-term mental health problems seeks to introduce community-oriented therapeutic activities. This could increase residents' self-determination while elevating the home's role within the community.

EXAMPLE 3
A residential children's social worker seeks to introduce a shared care scheme between families and the residential unit. This could assist in relationship building and genuine partnership work with parents and offer children more quality time with parents rather than being permanently in care.

EXAMPLE 4
A senior carer in a residential home for older people reviews the cyclical demand for beds. This might allow for greater proactive planning, proper resource provision and a differentiation of the needs for respite or full-time bed occupancy within specified time limits. This in turn might lead to an increase in resident/carer demand and satisfaction, as well as boosting profits.

The above examples are based on real-life appraised situations. The question that might be asked is what features contribute to their success? These features are as follows:

- Area for appraisal is kept simple.
- Area chosen is based on fair negotiation.
- Staff are empowered to identify areas within their current job descriptions and to focus on what they actually do or could do with support.
- There is realistic objective setting, which satisfies both individual and organisational needs.
- Methods for implementation are agreed.
- Paper exercises are avoided because they are too time-consuming.
- Appropriate times for review and evaluation are agreed.
- There is payment by result. The type of payment is decided in advance (it could be in the form of additional paid annual leave, or specialised training, etc.).

What if...?

If you now consider that an appraisal system is appropriate to your own career progression, as well as your individual and organisational needs, identify those features you consider necessary to ensure that a formalised appraisal scheme might work for you.

Why do some appraisal schemes fail?

Having developed an understanding of appraisal, and established a case for its use, as well as those features likely to ensure its success, let us now focus our attention on reasons why some appraisal schemes fail. Perhaps the most common are:

- a failure to train experienced appraising care managers;
- poor design and a lack of planning and preparation before implementation;
- a failure to involve staff from the outset, in the programme design;
- a failure to involve staff in identifying realistic targets (in other words targets are pre-set);
- too great a paper culture (such schemes are rarely sustainable, particularly if they require ongoing written inputs from others);
- a failure to set review dates to measure progress;
- a focus on personality traits rather than attainable employment-based targets;
- the use of appraisal as a method of social control, akin with a disciplinary process (this is less likely to win the favour of staff or to give them ownership of the process).

CASE STUDY — Appraisal

You are a care manager working for a charitable housing association that provides sheltered and assisted accommodation for older persons within a village setting. The targets you have set yourself for your appraisal are to reduce the high levels of staff turnover and increase and sustain motivation within the existing team structure.

- Identify those features of appraisal that are more likely to inhibit your scheme and may contribute to its failure.

- Identify those features most likely to contribute to its success.

Reflect on practice

List the appraisal skills you have already attained and those skills that would have to be developed. Prioritise the skills not yet attained and seek external formal training, additional supervision with a line manager or peer supervision with an experienced appraising colleague. Then repeat the exercise.

Performance appraisal – the skills and the benefits

An improvement in an organisation's overall performance is likely to incur cost and does need to be appropriately managed to achieve best practice. Clearly, staff development, which is an outcome of appraisal, is a major cost. Therefore, the appraising care manager should be able to demonstrate competence as:

- an effective communicator/negotiator;
- a sound planner;
- a trainer/adviser;
- an effective monitor of practice;
- a supporter;
- an attentive listener;
- an enabler of others;
- an organiser;
- a motivator;
- a coordinator.

If care managers are unable to demonstrate these skills, then they are likely to fail in their task and directly deny the organisation any growth from this innovative form of work. However, if the focus is upon simple, realistic and achievable outcomes of the five-stage approach to appraisal, then the advantages speak for themselves. These include:

- promotion of employee ownership of organisational goals and own role;
- direct participation of staff in the organisation;
- improvements in organisational development and quality of care;
- the meeting of employees' career aspirations;
- improvements in levels of service and the satisfaction of service users;
- greater loyalty and commitment from staff;
- more shared and accountable responsibility to get the job done;
- higher pay, promotion and upward career development for staff;

- opportunities for greater productivity, higher profit margins and greater visibility in a competitive marketplace for the organisation;
- an increased repertoire of skills and active management for care managers;
- a reduction in the remoteness of the management role.

The potential benefits of appraisal outweigh the costs. It does not demand another level of management, as it can take place within the existing care manager–employee relationship. Furthermore, if managed fairly, it could serve to strengthen this professional relationship, in which case everyone benefits.

3.3 Making presentations

Making oral presentations to either small or large groups is a powerful tool in the repertoire of skills you need to possess. There are specific techniques that turn this means of information exchange into both an individual and interactive experience. This section focuses on these techniques in order to facilitate best practice through the use of presentations to other people.

A presentation is a unique way of conveying information, to inspire and share best practice with team members. To ensure the communication achieves its desired outcome, there are a number of ground rules to follow. These relate to:

- preparation;
- presentation structure;
- performing;
- using new technology.

Preparation

No amount of charisma can replace the benefits of good planning and preparation for a presentation. The most important part of your preparation is to be clear about the message you want to give. You must have a good understanding of the content and any issues that are likely to arise. Sound planning and preparation would include most, if not all, of the following points:

- Consider the size of group you wish to make your presentation to. Is the information suitable for the size of audience?
- Book a suitable venue. Keep a written record of this!
- Ensure the environment offers sufficient space, lighting, heating, seating and air-conditioning. Additionally, make sure the physical structure is not distracting for the audience (columns/outside passing traffic, etc.).

- Consider time scales, attention span and any audience participation. Too much listening time can result in 'turn off'.
- Prepare your visual aids and hand-out material to match the content of your message (see also the section on the use of new technology, below).
- Consider the resources you need and unit cost your time as well as the actual cost of staff attending, and multiply this number if the same presentation has to be given to other groups.
- Always budget effectively in order that any presentation remains affordable.

Reflect on practice ••

Give examples of other kinds of preparation that need to be made for a presentation.

Presentation structure

The way you introduce your presentation is crucial. Too much detail or jargon without explanation at the start may result in your audience switching off. A short introduction that summarises the overall body of the subject matter should draw audience attention and prepare them to receive more information.

Always structure your presentation from concrete to abstract, that is, from simple to complex, in order to ensure that your audience remains alert to the stages of the information being presented. This will stop them 'getting lost' in the presentation. A fact sheet that maps the presentation from start to conclusion can be a useful tool. It also avoids the need to paraphrase and simply draws attention to the points covered or to be covered.

Reflect on practice ••

Consider when you were last in an audience. Try to remember what the speaker was conveying at the mid-point of the presentation.

If the presentation demands a practical demonstration, then audience participation becomes a prerequisite. They must be prepared for this in advance, their involvement massaged to such a point that when they are invited to participate there is a collective mood that encourages everyone to become involved in the 'whole experience'. This might be phrased as an audience 'attention stealer'.

Always recap on points made and conclude with a brief summary which draws the final elements together and offers, as a point of best practice, a thank you to all attending. On that note the presentation ends with your audience attention intact (in theory!).

What if...?

If you were to use some of the techniques you have experienced in other people's presentations, what would these be and what was it about them that facilitated your personal listening?

Performing

Dispel the myth! You do not have to be a charismatic performer to be an effective presenter. However, there are a number of skills, or powers, you will need to master to realise this role effectively and comfortably in public.

- *The power of your voice.* Why not listen to yourself speak using a portable tape recorder? It will help you to adjust the rate, tone, pitch and sound of your voice for critical emphasis.
- *The power of body language.* Your non-verbal communication (body stance and movements) can sometimes exert a more powerful influence than what you actually say. Consider whether it is better to sit, stand, move around or use hand gestures to attract audience attention. A video-recording of yourself can confirm your awareness of non-verbal communication.
- *The power of confidence.* If you are well prepared you will be more confident and less stressed.
- *The power of dress.* The clothes you wear for a presentation should meet the expected dress norms of your intended audience. Casual dressing can sometimes send mixed messages.
- *The power of expression.* Power of expression does not relate to how loud you can be; rather, it relates to whether you can convey your interest and involvement through controlled facial expression.
- *The power of consolidation.* Ensure that the rate, pitch and tone of your voice equate with your body language. The two forms of expression must always be in harmony and never in conflict.

Reflect on practice

How good are your performance skills? How might you change the manner of your delivery for future presentations?

An effective presenter always seeks to energise the audience by varying both pitch and tone of voice, encouraging participation by asking questions, employing practical demonstrations or using one of the many visual aids to grab that one special commodity, attention.

Using new technology

The technology you employ during a presentation can be as sophisticated as your presentation demands and as your audience expect. A practical demonstration involving using a hoist, an adjustable bed, or even a walk-in shower does, however, demand that these utilities are in place. However, a presentation based on aspects of practice can utilise an abundance of different aids, which, when used collectively, will help to maintain audience attention, assist their comprehension and enhance your presentation's effectiveness. Furthermore, images can also assist in delivering a particular point of view or help with a detailed explanation.

Some examples of new technology that can be used in the delivery of a presentation are discussed below.

Electronic presentations

Computer software, such as Microsoft PowerPoint, is essentially a form of slideshow presentation. You can connect your portable laptop computer to a digital projector to show images on a screen. The computer is activated by your voice via an infra-red remote-control mouse or via the keyboard. The attraction of this type of presentation is that it can remove the difficulty of body movement and the subsequent turning of your back on the audience. It also allows immediate and unconditional engagement by the facilitator, flexible eye contact and an acute awareness of non-verbal communication to gain audience attention.

Electronic presentations engage the audience on many levels

Furthermore, the technology offers sound and movement as part of the presentation, each of which can be used to hold attention or re-engage attention if there is a dip in the interest levels of the audience (usually mid-way through the presentation).

Interactive whiteboards

The whiteboard and pen can serve the function of a mouse but can also produce images on screen. Work can be shared, printed and immediately distributed. This technology is extremely user friendly as it minimises the risk of the audience becoming overwhelmed and allows everyone to be kept informed, while enabling some to catch up using diagrams or the written word.

WHITEBOARD WITH INDIVIDUAL HANDSETS

This is an extension of the interactive whiteboard that allows for an entirely interactive experience. The audience can use their individual handsets to contribute, which indirectly promotes audience participation and encourages the 'captive audience effect'.

Projector with video or DVD

This works on the principle of using multiple units plugged into your projector. In this way you may have the choice of using DVD (high-quality digital video), video-tape or your personal computer at any given time. The advantage that this type of presentation affords is the variety of media one can employ to maximum effect to capture audience attention. High-quality imagery increases audience attention and the use of variety provides stimulation.

Video-camera projecting images into the projector

This works simply by focusing your video-camera on individuals and projecting their images via the projector. It is an ideal tool to encourage focus as well as the use of humour in audience participation.

Digital camera

This extremely simple tool allows digital photographs to be taken of audience participative work or, for example, role modelling. The photographs can then be downloaded to a desktop or laptop computer and shown on a large screen.

Radio microphones

These two tools can be used separately or in tandem with your existing technological systems to boost your effectiveness as a presenter. A radio microphone consists of a small transmitter (some three and a half inches in length and two and a half inches in diameter), which can be attached to clothing, usually just above waist height. A thin wire is then attached discreetly to a small microphone, which can be hidden on a collar, lapel or tie, for example. The microphone is then adjusted to your natural voice level. This gives you the opportunity to convey your information without straining your voice, while retaining the ability to move around and be heard by everyone without inconvenience.

A hand-held radio microphone is just as simple. There are no transmitters or wires to concern yourself with; however, you are required to hold the microphone constantly below chin level. This demands some skill, as the natural inclination will be to hold it close to your mouth. The unfortunate outcome of this is that both the pitch and tone of your voice alter.

Both types of radio microphone have advantages and disadvantages. Which is chosen will come down to individual preference. Nevertheless, both allow you to be heard. Skilled presenters will maximise the use of these devices, particularly when making a presentation to a large group.

What if...?

If you were to use new technology to enhance the quality of presentations in your practice setting, which tools might best address your needs? Begin the prioritisation process.

CASE STUDY – Making presentations

You have recently been appointed care manager of a new, purpose-built, single-storey private residential home, which can accommodate some 50 residents. This new construction already complies with the Care Standards Act 2000 (namely Standards 19–25). Single-room capacity has been designed to meet the minimum of 12 square metres of usable floor space (excluding en suite facilities) required by 2007, even though existing units of this type have to be only 10 square metres. The Care Standards Act 2000 also imposes huge changes to staffing (Standards 27–30), management and administration (Standards 31–38), the health and personal care of residents (Standards 7–11), daily life and social activities (Standards 12–15) and complaints and protection (Standards 16–18). With a newly recruited staff group of some 60 personnel, you are aware that the presentation format can be used alongside other forums, such as supervision, team meetings and briefings, to deliver sometimes complex information, to whole teams or larger audiences, to maximise time, cost, staff learning and progression. How might you employ the presentation format as a constructive tool and technique to promote best practice?

● How will you begin to prepare yourself (and increase your confidence) and the content of your presentation, which will be to a mixed-ability staff group?

● What types of environment would be likely to engage your staff group?

● What will be the optimum size of group? Take into account how experienced you are in making presentations before reaching a decision.

● How will you resource multiple presentations and what kinds of financial planning skills will you require for this?

● How will you maximise your 'performing abilities'?

● What types of new technology will you consider experimenting with to enhance the quality of your presentations and subsequent staff learning, participation and comprehension?

● What methods of evaluating the outcome of your presentation(s) will you use?

3.4 Team briefings

The team briefing is an ideal forum in which to encourage team members to identify their developmental needs in order to achieve best practice for the organisation. This section therefore addresses formal and informal briefing structures; practice examples illustrate how both methods may be employed. The relationship between team briefings and individual development is explored through the operationalisation of two models: the self-assessment performance model and the self-development plan. Consideration is also given to the approaches to avoid, which either inhibit or residualise best practice, when in fact best practice should be readily achievable in this area.

Formal team briefings

These are pre-planned and have a fixed agenda and a set time scale. They will generally involve the whole team.

Practice example

A team briefing is held to address festive annual leave arrangements for Christmas and New Year. Team members to identify their specific individual needs. However, it is also necessary for them to be aware of organisational requirements and to ensure that residents' presenting needs are met.

Informal (or spontaneous) team briefings

These are not pre-planned. They often arise after a new referral, emergency admission or a change in service users' needs and care, about which the whole team needs to be briefed in order to provide the required care to expected standards of good practice.

Practice example

A couple with multiple disabilities and medical needs are newly referred for long-term care. The team needs to discuss and quantify the staffing time required to ensure that care can be provided 24 hours a day at a cost that is realistic yet achievable within present staffing quotas and budgets.

Reflect on practice

Consider the modes of briefings your practice setting adopts. Identify those which assist in meeting your personal developmental needs.

The relationship between team briefings and staff development

The briefing structure, whether formal or informal, allows team members to identify particular learning needs in relation to work plans and service users' needs. Two models are considered below that provide a framework for this: the self-assessment performance model and the self-development plan.

The self-assessment performance model

The self-assessment performance model shown in Figure 3.2 requires the team members to attend briefings and assess their own development needs in relation to work plans. It also promotes proactive objective setting and its possible impact on work plans with future service users. Individual learning style should also be taken into consideration.

The process allows the team member and manager to identify gaps or weaknesses with proposed work plans and to rectify through the development of new skills. Remember that a gap may be described as an area of service user dissatisfaction with specific elements of care, which may vary from lack of choice (e.g. in menu) to an inability to attend social activities as a result of a lack of awareness of mobility needs.

Self-assessment in line with the briefing structure enables the team member, in partnership with the service user, to take steps to learn new skills.

Figure 3.2 The self-assessment performance model

What if...?

If, as part of your briefing structure, you were to incorporate self-assessment as one means of identifying team members' weaknesses in objective setting and work planning, what would be the potential advantages to both individual and team performance in promoting a higher quality of resident care?

Self-development plan

The self-development plan, too, can be used within the framework of the team briefing structure to contribute towards meeting individual development needs. Again, a cycle emerges which enables team members to plan their own progress. There are five stages as shown in Figure 3.3.

To assess whether a self-development plan is realistic, it can be useful to use a 'SWOT' analysis – of strengths, weaknesses, opportunities and threats.

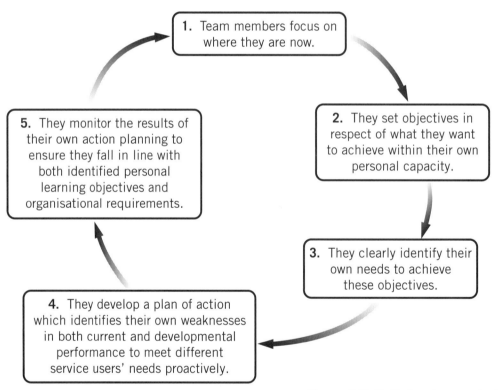

Figure 3.3 Self-development plan

Positive outcomes of both models

- Both models set out to identify shared goals of the individual, the team and the whole organisation.
- Both rely on developing learning objectives, which remain partly objective and partly subjective to self.

- The team briefing structure unifies and moulds individual and organisational needs and sets in motion a plan of action.
- Team members are very much in control of identifying their own needs and aspirations, as well as of planning and monitoring results.

Approaches to avoid

There are approaches to team briefings that are to be avoided if best practice is to be achieved.

Impose a solution

It is always best to rely on team members' creativity in identifying their own needs and solutions, without the requirement for imposition.

Manipulate

If the organisation puts its own needs first, it residualises team members' input.

Be unclear about the briefing structure

Be specific and accurate to ensure that team members' needs can be built upon. Anything less reduces the ethos of partnership.

CASE STUDY — Briefing and development

A formal team briefing identifies a series of gaps in moving from a 'white' model of residential living to a multicultural model of care. One of your staff group, Balbir, points out that all the residents are white and the culture of the organisation consequently caters only for the needs of a white resident group. The organisation ignores the needs of black and other ethnic minority groups who otherwise might avail themselves of specialised residential care.

- How might you begin to sensitise the staff group to consider developing a multicultural care model for meeting future needs?

- How might the introduction of a self-assessment model assist in essential objective setting and work planning with respect to cultural change?

- How might your team briefing structure be tailored to meet different team members' needs and to challenge prejudice?

- How might you encourage each member of staff to formulate a self-development plan to combat prejudice?

- How might you monitor progress?

3.5   Team-building activities

In order to achieve best practice, a commitment to ongoing team-building activities from the manager becomes a prerequisite. Team building by its nature is both a fluid and an exciting activity. It is your responsibility to ensure that it is matched to the team's actual stage of development and then extends beyond, in order to remain developmental.

This section focuses on eight team-building activities. These follow a natural progression, from the identification of aspirations and needs to the monitoring of outcomes. To that effect, best practice ceases to become unattainable and features as a reality that can become the norm of inspirational team building. The eight activities relate, respectively, to the following areas:

1 a sense of belonging;
2 team cohesiveness;
3 realistic roles;
4 maintenance functions;
5 shared team norms;
6 collective decision making;
7 an approach to team building;
8 monitoring progress.

The importance of team building

It is not unusual for teams to become frozen or stuck in their particular stage of development. Reasons for this are boundless – stagnation, lack of group maintenance, intergroup conflict, high staff turnover, or, quite simply, too many spiralists heading off in too many directions.

Team-building activities should become the norm of a team's working life if it is to continue to achieve best practice. It should also be remembered that team building should not be regarded as a panacea for bad practice. In essence, it remains simply a management tool for developing both individual and collective practice in unison. Therefore, it must be practical, comprehensible and, most importantly, achievable. Moreover, the process should never stop. It can take on various guises to energise group dynamics, including away-days, collective events or structured team problem-resolving days. Spontaneity in this regard will help to develop and maintain a team's balance; spontaneity is one of the hidden secrets of team building.

Activity 1. A sense of belonging

A manager who genuinely wishes team members to work interdependently must create a sense of belonging. This can be achieved only if members are taught to trust and support each other, and to be cooperative and mutually interactive. In an unattractive team, belongingness is not a right but a premium; this will lead to 'exit'. If groups work in competition and members of staff experience intolerable and unreasonable demands, then staff turnover will be high.

Therefore an intrinsic part of team building is to teach support, mutual trust and a belief system which constitutes ' I matter' and 'we matter collectively'. Then and only then will staff wish to belong to a team, which is there for them unconditionally, with no hidden agendas.

Reflect on practice

Identify the strengths and weaknesses within your existing team structure. Then consider what changes might be made in order to enhance a culture of belonging.

Activity 2. Team cohesiveness

Team-building activities should aim to develop team cohesiveness. The following suggestions are made to promote best practice.

- Encourage trust among members. If people do not trust each other, how can they realistically be expected to work together?
- Promote opportunities for professional friendships, underpinned by genuine interest, respect, trust and support.
- Ensure the team has the necessary resources (i.e. people, time, money and expertise) to carry out its functions.
- Reduce the role of competition in the drive for higher levels of performance.
- Whatever team structure is in place, whether vertical, horizontal or self-directed, ensure that the notions of equality and respect are prerequisites for all members.
- Acknowledge work well done and uphold the expertise and abilities of individual team members.
- Collective team accomplishment must be acknowledged and rewarded. This does not need to be a monetary incentive: more often a simple 'thank you' can grant a greater sense of worth.

How successful team-building activities are at developing team cohesiveness can be evaluated by the degree to which they achieve the following:

- shared objectives and a common goal;
- a sense of belonging;
- a sense of unity;
- a shared sense of success.

Once pulled together, the team unites in its belief system

There are three general benefits of team cohesiveness:

● Collective team morale is elevated.
● Teams can be managed more easily as they will identify and prioritise their own goals.
● Performance will focus upon the realistic rather than the unreasonable.

What if...?

If you were to consider developing a culture of closer team cohesiveness, what might be your priorities, and how would you implement them?

Activity 3. Realistic roles

Establishing realistic roles for team members is essential whenever a team:

● sets new objectives;
● creates new individual responsibilities;
● changes its functions;
● reorganises within the organisation;
● enlarges to accommodate new members.

To begin the process of analysing team members' roles, it is of great importance to clarify the work of the whole team and then to break it down into its component parts.

PRIORITIES FOR THE CARE MANAGER

- Clarify and draw up an individual work description for each team member.
- Identify individual team members' skills and expertise.
- Ensure there is no skills imbalance in relation to team-based priorities.
- Identify the skills and expertise that the team will need to meet its future obligations.
- Ensure that team members are aware of their own roles and responsibilities and, equally, those of other members.
- Identify the expectations of team members in relation to their contributions to the whole team, as well as in relation to their own professional development and career progression.
- Review roles regularly, as part of supervision. Where possible, extend responsibility, the expertise and new learning of team members, especially when team priorities change.

Reflect on practice

Undertake a work analysis of your own role. What skills do you possess and what skills will you require for future progression?

Activity 4. Maintenance functions

Awareness of group processes and of where individuals fit in relation to these dynamics is an effective way to minimise group conflict and fragmentation. Maintenance functions requires you to review the tasks members perform and their interrelationship with team working and the development of the individual within the team as a whole. Simultaneously, you must have an awareness of how group process affects the individual and be able to determine whether members belong to or are detached from the team. Additionally, there is a requirement for the care manager to promote professional working relationships among team members, not only for task achievement purposes but also to maintain group harmony. In this way dysfunction is easily identified and can be dealt with. Coolness and discretion should be employed to remove the risks of confrontation.

Team maintenance must also address the level of trust and security the team members feel towards each other. Best practice will put trust of others to the test, given the demands of a generic care setting. Maintenance is also about promoting a sense of group responsibility for self and others and recognition that membership of a team carries responsibility and accountability to the group.

In conclusion, maintenance skills within team building must be directed at an interpersonal level as well as at a team level. The outcome must be competent service delivery which meets service users' needs and thereby achieves best practice.

Reflect on practice

Consider the ways in which you manage complex interpersonal feelings yet also respond to team needs. How do you differentiate your feelings?

Activity 5. Shared team norms

Team-building activities must address team norms if they become dysfunctional. The norm of behaviour becomes the standard by which individual team members are expected to conform. Strong influences by more dominant members can exact pressure to conform even when the presenting behaviour is known to be wrong.

Tuckman (1965) refers to 'norming' as one of a sequence of stages in his model of group development. Ideally, it is a resolution of any confusion or conflict within the team. This ideal outcome should transpire in members bonding, consulting, supporting and demonstrating those cohesive qualities already explored within activity 2.

When team norms and management norms result in conflict, immediate intervention must take place.

Team-building activities can assist in the establishment of appropriate norms if the following steps are taken by the care manager:

- Identify the behaviours causing the problem.
- Identify staff or managers intentionally or unintentionally perpetuating these behaviours.
- Reduce the fear factor.
- Establish and enforce the behaviours that are contractually required of all staff.
- Observe and review occupational and verbal interactions between staff and management to discern unacceptable behaviours.
- Remove the sarcasm, inadequate information or threats or sanctions that potentially residualise staff in their role.
- Evaluate progress unconditionally, since the above behaviours damage service delivery and the integrity of the entire organisation.

Once in place, this simple form of team-building intervention can reduce established anxieties and return the team and organisational norms to a more harmonious and manageable position.

Team-building activities must seek to create a situation where team norms and organisational norms work in tandem for the protection of members, service users and the organisation, and not in competition.

What if...?

If, as team leader, you were faced with a small group of staff who suddenly began to defy team norms, how might you intervene?

Activity 6. Collective decision making

Collective decision making remains the essence of team-building activities, as each member contributes to the final result (see Figure 3.4).

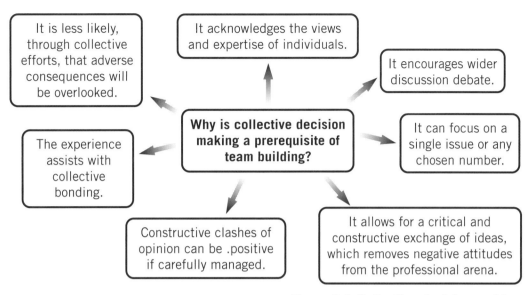

Figure 3.4 Collective decision making

Such decision making takes place within forums such as:

- team meetings;
- team briefings;
- hand-over meetings;
- problem-resolution meetings;
- structured team away-days.

Ideally, collective decision making would be contemplated when information is required from an extensive range of people, when different opinions can elevate understanding and the eventual decision has a direct impact upon the work of the team, and especially when the decision can be operationalised only by the collective body of the staff team.

There are disadvantages to collective decision making, however (see Figure 3.5).

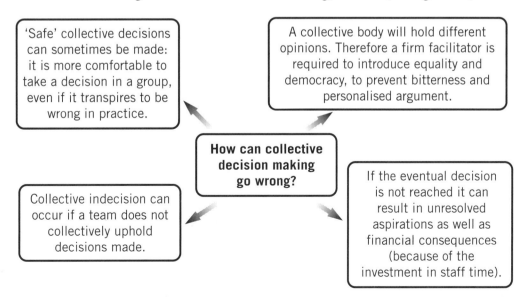

Figure 3.5 The disadvantages of collective decision making

It would be cynical to presume that these disadvantages outweigh the advantages of collective decision making, and to favour independent, individual decisions taken by management. Empowering group involvement can improve group dynamics and encourage the individual to work with and for the team. Equally, it can encourage the team to be responsive to individual needs.

CASE STUDY — Timekeeping

You are a care manager of a 25-bed private residential care home. Your care staff number some 15 personnel, who work in three teams supported by a senior carer to operate a 24-hour total care system. However, over the last three weeks you have noticed that there has been a shortfall of people turning up for the morning shift (7.30 am to 3.30 pm). This is placing both staff and residents at risk, which is intolerable and illegal under the Health and Safety Act 1974 and the Care Standards Act 2000. To resolve this situation you have called an obligatory staff meeting of all three teams.

- How will you word your statements to ensure there is group recognition of the problem. Give examples.

- How might you encourage the help of and contributions from the group?

- How might you differentiate individual from group problems?

- What manner must you adopt for the meeting?

- How will you avoid diffusion of responsibility or scapegoating?

- How will compromises be agreed with the group?

- What kinds of agreement might you consider satisfactory? How will you unite the group to ensure that the decision is followed?

- With a collective decision made, what forms of supervision might you suggest to preserve unity?

- How will you end the meeting so that staff can leave it without feeling bitter or resentful?

Activity 7. An approach to team building

The Woodcock nine-dimensional building block activity is a popular method of team building because its simplicity renders it successful. Woodcock (1986, p. 22) describes the characteristics or building blocks he employs as:

- clear objectives;
- openness and confrontation;
- support and trust;
- cooperation and conflict;
- sound procedures;
- appropriate leadership;
- regular reviews;
- individual development;
- sound intergroup relations.

These building blocks become a method of prioritising actual and potential difficulty. They clearly do not represent the only or definitive forms of potential dysfunction that a team is likely to face. However, they are examples of routine dysfunction.

The team-building programme uses an accompanying exercise manual to identify areas of central difficulty. You should work with the team for an agreed period of time, evaluate progress and move on. In this way a team continues to focus upon the individual within the group and fosters a group identity.

A team is not expected to work with all nine building blocks simultaneously. If a team were able to undertake such a task, it would not require the kinds of development that Woodcock suggests. In short, all that is required of a team is that it begins to practise as a group and to prioritise its needs.

Ideally, a team need only prioritise two or three central elements of dysfunction that it can manageably but intensively work on over a pre-set period of time. They might fall within the building block system or equally without. At one level, it may not matter because any area chosen is central to the development of the team and its collective contribution to the overall goals of the organisation, irrespective of type or specialism.

This approach to team building is task centred. It operates on the basis of encouraging individuals as well as the group to agree realistic targets for achievement and progression purposes. This approach, hypothetically, encourages any team to have ownership of its own targets, work with them collectively, evaluate performance of both self and peers, measure and quantify progress, re-prioritise and move on.

The Woodcock building block system represents a very simple tool for anyone committed to team building, and it embodies the principles that best practice demands. It might be reasonably argued that embodying principles of best practice and achieving them represent two different outcomes. Nevertheless, this system allows for both and can be reasonably advocated by management taking the lead and role modelling the very same principles. In this way, the team can similarly mirror, role model, copy by example, bond and move forward optimistically.

CASE STUDY — Encouraging support and trust

You have recently been appointed care manager of a multidisciplinary private care provider that has a residential home that accommodates 60 people, a thriving day centre that offers some 40 places and a local community care service that supports some 80 service users in their own homes. This service you estimate increases by some 10% each month. You recognise that the three-tier team structure is very fragile as an outcome of short-term successive managers combined with a high turnover of staff. Stability needs to be restored and support and trust among management and staff is a high priority. Under these very sensitive conditions, how might you proceed?

- List the changes you will attempt to introduce to create a culture of openness and proactive support.

- Why might you establish time limits for collective review and measurement of progress?

- At the end of your negotiated period, why is it so important to engage in a collective evaluation of progress?

- If you consider that circumstances have stabilised as a result of this form of intervention, how will you move forward and what future targets might you renegotiate and set for progression purposes? List some targets for short-, medium- and long-term developments?

Activity 8. Monitoring progress

Monitoring progress of both team activity and progression on an ongoing basis is essential in order that individual/group commitment to negotiated objectives and targets remains on track. However, monitoring group dynamics is a difficult task and unlike measuring the results of a production or commodity line. It might be worthwhile to review performance with your team by asking a few specific questions:

- What have we negotiated?
- Where are we currently?
- How near are we to meeting our current targets?
- What routes or alternatives should we consider to arrive at our predetermined destinations?

A team achievement plan will aid the process of monitoring. This involves writing a series of questions which relate to any objectives or targets. The plan will need to be reviewed regularly, say weekly or fortnightly, as team needs dictate. A rating scale (e.g. 1–10) can be introduced, with 1 representing poor or depressing and 10 representing excellent (see the example of a team achievement plan below). The plan must remain fluid as the subject is a matter of constant review. However, the key to success is to set a target whereby four to five points are improved at each review, making this task manageable and achievable.

Team Achievement Plan

Rate each point 1 to 10, 1 representing depressing and 10 representing excellent.

Also similarly rate overall achievement.

Rating (1 to 10)

- All team members are aware of the objective they have agreed. ☐

- All team members maintain a sense of openness and trustworthiness. ☐

- All team members have a skills mix to achieve pre-set objectives. ☐

- Regular review helps the team to measure actual progress. ☐

- All team members contribute their expertise to achieve pre-set objectives. ☐

- All team members contribute towards collective leadership style. ☐

- All team members have a mutual responsibility to support each other. ☐

- The team has the right to resolve its problems and make new decisions. ☐

- All team members have the right to contribute to the decision-making process. ☐

- The team has the right to plan ahead for progression purposes. ☐

Example of a team achievement plan.

The team development plan can be simply described as a management tool which encourages participation, energises the team and commits individuals to a collective team process of decision making, aimed at team development. The outcome must be to achieve best practice. In this way the team as a whole is capable of performing and by regular review can measure its progress towards achieving its desired objectives.

3.6 Involvement and motivation of team members

Best practice demands the involvement and motivation of team members in proactive objective setting and work planning. This section begins by differentiating between commitment and compliance, and explores positive and negative outcomes in relation to both objective setting and work planning. It then briefly looks at some theoretical constructs of motivation. The section then examines the setting of objectives, the work plan and the developmental needs plan and their combined usefulness in achieving best practice.

Commitment versus compliance

Winning the commitment of team members to proactive objective setting and work planning is not the same as gaining their compliance. Commitment is a direct result of ownership and personal involvement. It is more likely than mere compliance to generate new ideas, realistic objectives and achievable work plans. Consequently, commitment should improve the productivity and retention of staff.

Compliance, on the other hand, tends to yield the opposite. It is likely to be associated with a culture of blame, where management takes little responsibility and with team members performing only at a minimum level, to avoid blame. They still comply and do what is demanded; however, their work efforts and throughputs are likely to fall short of achieving the results that objective work planning requires.

What motivating influences are required to win commitment and thereby motivate team members to engage in proactive objective setting and work planning, to achieve best practice? Three examples are considered below.

Professional working relationships

As care manager, it is advisable that you get to know your team members both professionally and personally. Encourage two-way communication in order that mutual qualities can be shared, mirrored and experienced. Trust, support and mutual understanding should become the norm for professional relationships.

It is important to encourage two-way communication in professional relationships

Team member ownership

Encourage team member initiative by delegating responsibility for task achievement. Support their involvement, as effective delegation is underpinned by responsible supervision and you will remain accountable for task achievement. Accountability is non-negotiable and remains a management remit, but there is nonetheless a need for unconditional team member ownership of objective setting for work planning purposes.

Autonomy and accountability

The challenge is to ensure a stimulating yet developing working environment. This can be achieved by encouraging a culture of combined team member autonomy and accountability, in unison. The outcome has to be measured in terms of commitment to task achievement, in return. Commitment is more likely where there are good staff retention levels, appraisal of work undertaken, satisfied service users and elevated levels of morale; these will also increase the quality of care provided, irrespective of the practice setting.

Reflect on practice

How do you professionally differentiate between the importance of commitment and a legal mandate for compliance to the Care Standards Act 2000 within your practice setting? Give examples to support your response.

What if...?

If you were required to increase team motivation and commitment, to encourage mutual support and accountability for work planning initiatives, what methods might you employ? Jot down your thoughts on this highly important team management matter.

CASE STUDY — Staff retention problems

You are a care manager of a regional charity which specialises in offering residential care, community support and training for future employment opportunities for individuals with learning disabilities. The organisation has embraced the Care Standards Act 2000. In particular, you have put in place personal staff training/qualification contracts, in compliance with Standard 28.1 of the Act, for all care staff. However, once staff have been trained to mandatory NVQ level 2, you experience difficulty in retaining them. How do you resolve this investment crisis in staff development and maintain the calibre of personnel?

- What new challenges might you offer trained staff to NVQ level 2?
- How could you increase team member ownership and commitment to their role within the organisation?
- How could you encourage team member autonomy and accountability?
- What measures might you employ to motivate team members, to improve staff retention, in particular after they have qualified?

Theoretical constructs of motivation

So much research has been done in this field that the care manager is spoilt for choice. The humanistic schools began with Mayo, and the neo-humanists extended this tradition. Included among the latter is Maslow (1953), with his motivational pyramid based on five levels of meeting basic needs, to the point of self-actualisation. This theory operates on the assumption that unless team members' basic presenting needs are met, they will not self-actualise or realise their full ability. In essence, it is a classical building block approach based on meeting lower-level needs before being able to work through the hierarchy.

Herzberg's hygiene theory of motivation, by contrast, focuses on job satisfaction rather than work-based fulfilment (Herzberg *et al.*, 1960). In essence, he separates what he considered motivators, which empower staff performance, and satisfiers, which equate with a sense of achievement and a feeling of recognition. Dissatisfiers, or hygiene factors, may equate with conditions of work, although salary is not the main issue here.

Both these theories use a hierarchical breakdown. In contrast, another approach, called Theory X and Theory Y (McGregor, 1960), operates on the assumption that a care manager will behave differently to team members based on preconceived assumptions about members' ability and performance. Theory X focuses on the 'iron hand' method of motivation – the use of authority, rules, threats or even blame. Theory Y focuses on the incentive method of motivation, which might include payment by results (i.e. performance-related pay), a company car or free private health insurance. It might be suggested that while theory Y is the ideal method of motivation, at some point in the process of care management resort to theory X becomes inevitable. Hence there needs to be a balance between the two.

The research of Yetton and Vroom (1978) and Lawler and Porter (1968) has given rise to 'expectancy theory'. This theory of motivation is based on how a team member might recognise that effort improves performance, which in turn can lead to reward. Its rationale is based on whether team members' motivation to perform is dependent on what they expect to derive from the task. An evaluation by the team member is made of how much effort should be expended on the task, against the value in terms of reward.

The four theories presented above are not definitive but offer a theoretical construct of what team motivation is about and what it might achieve in practice.

Reflect on practice •

Consider how the theories of Maslow, Hertzberg and McGregor interrelate. Give examples drawn from your own experience.

What if...?

If you had to introduce a series of motivational incentives to enhance the work efforts of your team, how might their success be measured?

CASE STUDY — The demotivated team

You are newly appointed manager of an NHS primary care community-based project that offers support to the families of people who suffer from a mental illness. You recognise that a well-motivated multidisciplinary team is more likely to achieve its goals. However, you find that team members are reluctant to engage in any proactive objective setting or work planning with service users or their families, and look to you for constant direction. How might you reverse this trend?

- Why might you need to explore the past history of this team?

- What methods might you employ to ensure your team feels motivated?

- How might you increase team members' job satisfaction?

- What additional measures might you adopt to support team members' autonomy and commitment to both role and task.

Effective objective setting and work planning as a means of involving and motivating team members

Objective setting and work planning can be effective only if you, as care manager, can differentiate between current ability and the developmental needs of your staff. Objective setting and work planning might focus upon knowledge, skills and accredited qualifications. By contrast developmental needs focuses upon the preparation required to fulfil new roles and tasks for both professional and organisational development. You must motivate team members to engage in consistent objective setting and work planning that take into account current and developmental needs.

The case study 'Objectives and work plans' highlights the need for open discussion by all parties involved in the process of both objective setting and work planning. Only then can the expressed needs of service users and team members be met and levels of motivation maintained, thus demonstrating best practice in each aspect of care management.

CASE STUDY — Objectives and work plans

Harjit is 79 years of age and has been a resident for some six months. He was originally admitted as a single person who was not self-caring and who required renal dialysis once a week at a local NHS trust hospital. The previous objectives and work plans had been designed to empower mobilisation and self-autonomy. His key worker, Jasbir, had supervised this programme of care with the help of two other members of the team. Both the objective setting and the delivery of the work plan have succeeded. Now Harjit wishes to resume both religious and cultural activities at his local temple.

The objectives
Facilitate requested religious and cultural activities by networking with local Sikh community, temple elders and community volunteers.

The work plan
Jasbir to network with temple volunteers to arrange transport as well as invite them to visit Harjit in his own setting, to identify those particular activities he wishes to pursue within the temple. Additionally, Jasbir to consult Harjit over his wishes and preferences.

The key worker, Jasbir is a senior carer and an experienced residential care worker, qualified to NVQ 3 in care. He has developed, in partnership with his team, a programme aimed at developing awareness and sensitivity to the different physical, cultural and religious needs of the local Sikh and Hindu communities. As a result of Harjit's admission, he undertook the coordination role with his team of supervising Harjit's in-house mobilisation programme as well as consolidating team-based cultural knowledge. He has personally requested to supervise the new work plan, to delegate essential roles and tailor it specifically to meet Harjit's wishes, to preserve his own sense of personal autonomy.

Developmental needs plan
Jasbir needs to raise the cultural awareness, knowledge and skills of his team to work with Asian residents and meet their different needs. Jasbir's own developmental needs will include opportunities to develop team-based skills of networking, of delegating work, of supervision and overall coordination.

- How might you approach Harjit's expressed preferences without a knowledge of Sikh culture?

- How might you raise awareness and show how cultural barriers can be overcome?

- Is the work plan sufficient to meet Harjit's expressed needs and preserve his own sense of personal autonomy? If not, suggest some alternatives.

- Does the work plan provide sufficient professional development opportunities for Jasbir and his team?

- Are the objectives for the new work plan too ambitious to meet Harjit's newly presenting needs?

Summary

The outcome of formulating realistic policies and practices, using the correct tools and techniques, must be to attain the most effective teamwork practice. However, to sustain such collective inter-group relations and develop its overall practice to achieve qualitative resident care, it becomes imperative to supervise both individual and team practices. Supervision must be seen as a process rather than an event. Its aims should be kept simple and realistic to improve team members' occupational role, nurture responsibility, accountability, and support, and assist in achieving organisational goals, irrespective of the work setting.

Appraisal is another method to sustain best team practice. Its role is to focus on measuring team member strengths and weaknesses through realistic target setting against the key outcome areas of role. Therefore the mission that appraisal seeks to realise, albeit in a tripartite way, is to improve service user care, organisational development and further member career aspirations. The team briefing structure is also an ideal forum to encourage members to identify and assess their own developmental needs in order to action required work plans.

A prerequisite of achieving best practice is a commitment to ongoing developmental team building. Its nature should be kept both fluid and exciting to address the team's actual stage of development. In this way, team building focuses upon the natural processes of aspirational need and the required monitoring of progress.

Last but not least, best practice can be achieved through the involvement and motivation of team members by engaging in pro-active objective setting and work planning. The manager's role is to identify the team member's current ability and his or her developmental needs. If both are supervised and regularly appraised, then it is more likely they will remain consistent with current and future occupational roles required to meet different resident needs.

Check your knowledge

1 What do you think supervision means?

2 What do you expect from supervision? Prioritise your ideas.

3 List the types of supervision you would prefer to access in your work environment and why.

4 Explain why appraisal is a prerequisite of best practice? Give examples.

5 Try to recall previous presentations you have attended. Select one which engaged your attention and explain why.

6 Consider how new technology might enhance the quality of your future presentations and participant comprehension within your practice setting. Identify which tools are likely to assist in this process.

7 Drawing on your own experience, identify which mode of team briefing is more likely to assist in meeting personal/developmental needs and why.

8 What does successful team building involve? List three key points.

9 How might you suggest employing the Woodcock team development system within your practice setting, given the stage development of your team? Could this system assist in the removal of interpersonal barriers to enable the team to work more as a group? If so, how?

10 How does your practice setting encourage meaningful objective setting and work planning which meets service user needs? What additional system of review might be made to ensure success? Give examples.

Appendix 3.1 Supervision checklist

Before supervision I will:

♦ Book a room which affords maximum privacy and confidentiality.

♦ Prepare the room in advance to avoid physical barriers or too many distractions.

♦ Ensure the chairs allow for ergonomic support and comfort.

♦ Arrange for availability of refreshments.

♦ Inform colleagues that I am not available, to avoid disruption.

♦ Check the agenda.

♦ Keep to the agreed arrangements unless there is an overriding and negotiated reason to do otherwise.

To prepare myself I will:

♦ Review supervisory notes made previously, to refresh my memory.

♦ Check the agenda already negotiated. Ensure supervisees' suggestions are there and that copies are given out.

♦ Ensure that any documentation or materials I promised are available.

♦ Check the time available against the length of the agenda and make any necessary allowances for this.

During supervision I will:

♦ Greet supervisees and put them at ease.

♦ Check and agree the agenda with supervisees.

♦ Ensure we have all the materials and information required.

♦ Open the conversation by quickly summarising where we are.

♦ Enable supervisees to discuss own areas and issues.

♦ Prompt and/or question if necessary.

♦ Encourage a relaxed but focused attitude.

♦ Use humour constructively.

♦ If supervisees are reluctant to talk, use icebreakers.

♦ Use silence positively and not get embarrassed.

♦ Move on with focus and act non-defensively.

♦ Not allow myself to be threatened.

♦ Assert myself when appropriate.

♦ Identify problem areas.

♦ Enable supervisees to find own solutions. If not, offer advice.

♦ Not allow the discussion to wander. Keep to the point.

♦ Ask open-ended questions.

♦ Listen actively to responses.

♦ Admit my limitations, where I am unable to respond to a question.

♦ Recognise that I too am here to learn.

♦ Accept that supervision is a two-way learning experience.

♦ Accept that total responsibility does not lie with me.

♦ Accept I am accountable for facilitating and recording the process.

♦ Question whether I have problems with this role and learning and experience.

♦ Summarise and paraphrase where necessary to test comprehension.

♦ Record decisions made at the time.

♦ Encourage the same of supervisees, for mutual accountability.

At the end of supervision I will:

♦ Draw together the threads of the discussion.

♦ Test comprehension of key points.

♦ Identify what will be discussed in the next session.

♦ Identify what materials need to be brought, and by whom, to the next session.

♦ Fix an appropriate date, time and place for the next session.

♦ Finish on a relaxed note so that we can resume our duties feeling a sense of achievement as an outcome of the session.

Appendix 3.2 Example of a supervision record

Victoria Seasons – Private Residential Home for Older People

Name of supervisee: David Thomas (Senior Carer)
Name of supervisor: Alison Ward (Care Manager)
Date: 16/08/03
Time: From 1pm to 2pm
Date of last supervision: 15/07/03.

Issues carried over from last supervision

Supervisee   Workload – Key residents to be reduced from 8 to 6 to maintain quality care.
Staff on shift – A minimum of 5 care workers, plus a senior on every shift,
with domestic and kitchen support.

Supervisor   Review workload in light of current and projected number of residents in
the next financial quarter.
Review staff quotas in light of David's request and Social Care
Commission advised minimum standards.

Issues raised in this session

Supervisee   Workload, staffing, incentives, training.

Supervisor   Workload, staffing and developmental staff training for all.

Summary of meeting

Areas discussed – workload, staffing, and incentives, pay and time off in lieu, and paid
salary for contractual training.

Decisions made – key workers to work with no more than 6 residents individually,
providing staff levels remain consistent. Day care unit to be managed separately. A
senior carer to be appointed on every shift. To be appointed from within existing staff
teams. Kitchen and domestic staff to remain the same.

Training – All staff training to be addressed via a skills audit of needs to meet local and
National Care Standards. All staff to be interviewed by David and Alison in the next two
weeks. Once overall picture emerges an action plan can be drawn up which prioritises
training for all, but will differentiate between 'in house' and external training.

Issues for next session

Report back on results of staff interviews. Organise a staff meeting to address outcome.
Put in place an action plan to meet needs as they present.

Any other business – none.
Date of next session: 17/09/03

Signed: *D. Thomas*   Dated: 16/08/03
Signed: *A. Ward*   Dated: 16/08/03

Appendix 3.3 An example of a supervisory recording of statutory child protection fieldwork practice

Supervisor: G. Woods

Supervisee: J. Smith

Date of supervision: 12/08/03

Name of child: C. Davies

Date of birth: 1/11/01

Address: Larch Crescent, Bradford

Computer number: _ _ _ _

Legal status: CPR (neglect)

Areas of discussion and action undertaken

1.1 ASSESSMENT AND CARE PLAN – To discuss case conference with parents separately and together. Begin care assessment involving play with child (use an assessment model of child development – Piaget, etc.).

1.2 CHILD'S WISHES (or observations in this case, as child too young) – Child seems to be isolated from parents, no toys observable, house is very cold. Both parents on methadone support. Parents have a history of not keeping medical appointments. Health visitor reports that child is not taken to clinic with a degree of regularity.

1.3 DISCUSSION OF TASKS TO BE ACHIEVED AND FREQUENCY OF VISITS – Core group of multidisciplinary professionals to commence meeting and parents to work with group collectively and agree plan.

1.4 PRIORITY AND DISCUSSION OF WORKER'S CAPACITY (LIMITATIONS) AND VARIETY OF NEEDS – Worker may have competing priorities or be on leave, off sick. Discuss how work will be delegated in that instance and outcome orientated. Any monitoring must be on a daily basis by supervisee or any other worker.

1.5 AGREED TASKS – CORE GROUP – Set date(s) in advance of planned social worker visits and those of care members, so parents have advanced warning. Clarify roles of agency involvement; ensure no duplication of work occurs. Also clarify parental roles in this process, what will they be working at and how to proceed (so that they know what they are doing). Consider alternatives if agreed plan fails.

1.6 RECORDING CHECKED ON FILES – Action by both (daily).

1.7 INFORMAL SUPERVISION – Throughout the week to ensure work is progressing and child is seen (observed) – action by both (daily).

1.8 DISCUSSION OF ANY DIFFICULTIES – For example Health and Safety etc. – action by both (daily).

Formal supervision: 4 weeks' time.

Informal supervision and essential monitoring: daily.

Signed 12/08/03

Signed 12/08/03

Appendix 3.4 Example of a record sheet for informal appraisal

Staff appraisal, School of Social Work

Management objectives for 2003/2004

♦ Essential training days for all staff – 4 days per academic year.

♦ All full-time and part-time lecturers to attain a recognised teaching qualification.

♦ All staff to be computer literate and obtain a CLAIT qualification.

♦ Opportunities for professional development – 5 days per year.

♦ Opportunities for either research or MA qualification – graduates only.

♦ Opportunities for industrial secondment – management decision.

Staff member's intended development

Priority areas:

Proposed date of attainment

♦ Spend time (5 days) with Northamptonshire SSD	September 2003
♦ Attend essential training on classroom observation	November 2003
♦ Attain CLAIT and other recognised IT qualifications	July 2004

Signature of staff member and date: *Jean Smith, 23/06/03*

Signature of head of school/faculty and date: *Ronald Allen, 23/06/03*

Appendix 3.5 Example of a written procedure for staff appraisal (five-stage approach)

The example below pertains to a nursing home.

♦ *Job content.* Care manager and employee to discuss current job description and the key outcome areas for which they are paid. Employee to choose one area which they feel they can improve.

♦ *Performance targets.* With area chosen, encourage employee to set a performance target that focuses upon customer, organisational and own career aspirations for actual improvement to current practice. Keep it simple, realistic and attainable.

♦ *Negotiation – employee centred.* Let them take control and own their chosen area. Listen to their views and comment only on the realism of chosen target and its potential impact on care practice. Identify what method of merit will be awarded upon completion and success.

♦ *Monitoring.* Set time limit of no more than three months for target area to be achieved. Listen to the employee's viewpoint. Identify review periods, for example weekly, fortnightly, etc. Encourage employee to identify what evidence they need to collate for each review session throughout the actual process. Fix dates, times and venue for each review session in advance.

♦ *Evaluating the outcome.* At the end of the quarter evaluate the whole process and key improvements which target area was set to achieve. This must be evidenced to include customer, organisational and employee need(s). If achieved, bestow merit award immediately.

References and further reading

Section 3.1

REFERENCES

Cusins, P. (1994) *Be a Successful Supervisor*. London: Kogan Page.

Drucker, P. F. (1988) *Management: Tasks, Responsibilities, Practices*. Oxford: Heinemann.

Pettes, D. E. (1979) *Staff and Student Supervision: A Task Centred Approach*. National Institute of Social Services Library.

FURTHER READING

Chapman Elwood, H. (1994) *The First Time Supervisor: A Guide for the Newly Promoted*. London: Kogan Page.

Evans, D. (2001) *Supervisory Management: Principles and Practice* (5th edition). London: Continuum International Publishing.

Hawkins, P. and Shohet, R. (2000) *Supervision in the Helping Professions. An Individual, Group and Organisational Approach*. Buckingham: Open University Press.

Pritchard, J. (1995) *Good Practice in Supervision: Statutory and Voluntary Organisations*. London: Jessica Kingsley.

Stone, B. (1991) *Supervisory Skills*. London: Pitman.

WEBSITES

Clinical supervision
www.clinical-supervision.com

Ironmill Institute
www.ironmill.info

Management supervision and leadership techniques
leadershipmanagement.com/html-files/manage.htm

Section 3.2

REFERENCES

Pettes, D. E. (1979) *Staff and Student Supervision: A Task Centred Approach*. National Institute of Social Services Library.

Mullins, L. (1999) *Management and Organisational Behaviour*, 5th edition. London: Pitman.

FURTHER READING

Cartwright, R. (1998) *Managing People: A Competence Approach to Supervisory Management*. Oxford: Blackwell.

Evans, D. (1999) *Supervisory Management: Principles and Practices*, 4th edition, Cassell.

Hunt, M. (1994) *How to Conduct Staff Appraisals*, 2nd edition. Oxford: How to Books.

Maddux, R. (1990) *Effective Performance Appraisals*. London: Kogan Page.

WEBSITES

Pert: Performance appraisal planning worksheet
orpheus.ucsd.edu/pert/other/tools/pertwksh.htm

Section 3.3

FURTHER READING

Berry, C. (2000) *Your Voice and How To Use It*, 2nd edition. London: Virgin.

Bessant, A. (2001) *Learning to Use PowerPoint: Creating Effective Presentations*. Oxford: Heinemann.

Burrows, T. (2000) *Creating Presentations.* London: Dorling Kindersley.

Hindle, T. (1998) *Essential Managers: Making Presentations.* London: Dorling Kindersley.

Jasmine, G. (2000) *Cliff Notes: Creating a Winning PowerPoint 2000 Presentation.* Chichester: John Wiley & Sons.

Kalish, K. (1997) *How to Give a Terrific Presentation.* New York: Amacom.

Rozakis, L. (1999) *The Complete Idiot's Guide to Public Speaking.* Indianapolis: Alpha Books.

Stevenson, N. (2003) *Create Microsoft PowerPoint 2002 Presentations in a Weekend.* Boston: Prima Tech.

Section 3.4

FURTHER READING

Deal, T. and Kennedy, A. (2000) *The New Corporate Cultures.* Harmondsworth: Penguin.

Forsyth, P. (1996) *Making Meetings Work.* CIPD.

Hodgson, P. (1992) *Effective Meetings,* ("The Sunday Times") Business Skills London: Random House Business Books.

Section 3.5

REFERENCE

Tuckman, B. W. (1965) 'Developmental sequence in small groups', *Psychological Bulletin*, vol. 63, p. 6.

Woodcock, M. (1986) *The Team Development Manual. Part 1, Improving Teamwork.* Aldershot: Gower.

FURTHER READING

ACAS (2003) *Teamwork: Success Through People*, ACAS.

Anderson, N., Hardy, G. and West, M. (1990) 'Innovative teams at work', *Personnel Management*, vol. 22, pp. 48–53.

Ford, C. (1994) *Teamwork – Key Issues*, ACAS.

Guzzo, R. A. and Shea, G. P. (1992) 'Group performance and integral relations', in M. D. Dunnette and L. M. Haugh (Eds), *Handbook of Industrial and Organisational Psychology*, 2nd edition, Consulting Psychologist Press.

Moxon, P. (1998) *Building a Better Team*, Gower.

Tjosvold, D. (1992) *Team Organization: An Enduring Competitive Advantage.* Chichester: Wiley.

WEBSITES

ACAS
    www.acas.org.uk

Groups that Work article
    www.see.ed.ac.uk/~gerard//Management/art0.html?http:/oldeee.see.ed.ac.uk//~gerard/Management/art0.htm1

Twelve Tips for Team Building
    http://humanresources.about.com/library/weekly/aa112501a.htm

The Team Resource Center
    www.team-creations.com/Teamwork.htm

Teambuilding Inc articles
    www.teambuildinginc.com/ei_news.htm

What Makes Teams Work?
    www.fastcompany.com/online/40/one.html

Section 3.6

REFERENCES

Herzberg, F., Mausler, B. and Synderman, B. (1960) *Motivation to Work*. Chichester: Wiley.

Maslow, A. H. and Frager, R. (1970) *Motivation and Personality*, Harper & Row.

Mayo, E. (2003) *The Human Problems of an Industrial Civilization*. London: Routledgee.

McGregor, D. (1960) *Human Side of Enterprise*. Maidenhead: McGraw-Hill.

Porter, L. W. and Lawler, E. E. (1968) *Managerial Attitudes and Performance*. Maidenhead: McGraw-Hill-Irwin.

Yetton, P. W. and Vroom, V. H. (1978) 'The Vroom–Yetton model of leadership – an overview', in B. King, S. Strenfert and F. E. Fieldler (Eds), *Management Control and Organisational Democracy*. Chichester: Wiley.

FURTHER READING

Armstrong, M. (1995) *Handbook of Personnel Management Practice*, 5th edition. London: Kogan Page.

Attwood, M. and Dimmock, S. (1996) *Personnel Management*, 3rd edition. Basingstoke: Macmillan.

Croft, S. and Beresford, P. (1990) *From Paternalism to Participation*, Open Services Project, Joseph Rowntree Foundation.

Evendon, R. and Anderson, G. (1992) *Management Skills: Making the Most of People*. Harlow: Addison-Wesley.

WEBSITES

Accel-team.com
www.accel-team.com/techniques/index.html

APPENDIX A

Leading teams in the 21st century

A.1 Becoming a 21st century leader

It is probably clear by now that leading and inspiring teams is not a matter of luck. It takes hard work, dedication and a sound knowledge of your organisation. Specific examples include:

- the law as it relates to your area of work
- dedication
- sensitivity
- high standards
- a willingness to continually increase your own knowledge and learning
- a willingness to enable others to develop their skills and knowledge
- sound human resources skills
- good delegation skills
- trust and honesty.

Being a good leader is not just a matter of seeing that the job gets done. It is also about knowing how to handle yourself and your staff to produce the best possible results. It is about being able to think flexibly, strategically and operationally as the work demands.

This Appendix contains suggestions that you can use for your continuing development outside the requirements of the NVQ. You can still use this material to obtain your award, but as a leader and manager of others you should be outward looking and constantly striving to improve your own knowledge and capabilities. Therefore, this part of the book is intended to provide some direction and further thoughts that you may wish to follow up. Worksheets and case studies have been included to help you think through your current and future development needs.

If you have already come across some of these ideas during higher level study, they should serve as reminders for good leadership. If the information is entirely new to you, it should be a springboard for further personal and professional development.

A.2 Strategic and operational management issues

Is there a difference between strategic and operational management? The short answer is yes! As time goes on, you are more likely to become involved in strategic decision making and planning for the future of your organisation. As the leader of your workplace or department, you may be expected to have views on its future performance and potential direction. For example, many care organisations are currently taking strategic decisions about whether to participate in intermediary care programmes, and predicting the effect of such programmes on their organisations.

Strategic management is about providing direction for the organisation or department. It supplies ways of achieving the organisation's vision, mission, values and objectives. Figure A.1 shows some ways of achieving successful strategies.

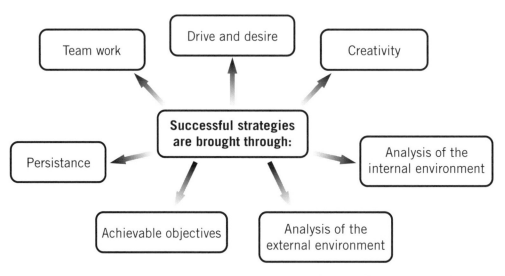

Figure A.1 Methods of achieving successful strategies

Interacting with others is essential for the creation of effective strategies. A good leader or manager will:

- use different interpersonal styles to help guide the team to completion of a task
- be assertive or even forceful, demonstrating a readiness for the task
- make a strong impact at first meetings

- have credibility
- persuade others to see his or her point of view
- inspire and motivate others
- show an understanding for the feelings of others
- be flexible through a willingness to listen and change, where necessary.

Operational management is more closely linked to the everyday activities that need to take place to ensure that an organisation's targets are met. Operational management can be at a high level or a lower level in the organisation

Visioning: a central part of leadership?

As part of strategic direction it is important that all leaders have a 'vision' and, from this, a 'mission' to follow. If you don't know where you're going, you'll never know when you've arrived!

In some health and care organisations, the vision and mission are developed for you. In others, you are asked to develop these with your team. However your vision and mission have been developed, now is a good time to review them. It might be useful to start by exploring the difference between a vision and a mission.

Vision

This is the leader's dream for the future of the department or organisation. It should:

- not be so precise that it cannot be refined or embellished
- lend itself to articulation so that it can be explained to other people
- inspire and empower others
- be achievable through translation into objectives and strategy
- make sense to clients and stakeholders
- be clear about its aim.

Mission

By contrast, the mission tends to be a statement about how the organisation is going to create 'value' for the service user and perhaps also their family members. The mission is about adding value to the service by offering something that the client can expect over and above the obvious services. Often, it concerns making people's lives seem better, and the product or service itself is not mentioned at all. So, in a health and social care context, the mission might be about better futures, peace of mind and so on.

What if...?

If you were asked for your vision and mission for your organisation, what would you say? Do you know where your organisation is going? If not, spend some time thinking about the purpose and direction required for the successful continuation of your organisation.

Values

Values are those things that don't change, even when everything else is changing in the organisation. Values provide stability; they could be seen as representing guidelines for when 'bad' things happen (for example, redundancies).

It is likely that the values of your organisation are based upon those of the Care Value Base. A values statement is likely to contain words such as:

- respect
- dignity
- confidentiality
- equality
- quality
- fairness
- sensitivity.

Many organisations have sets of values for their clients, staff and, in some cases, for the way management behaves to staff and service users.

CASE STUDY — Overview of management charter:

Green Glades Domestic Care Agency

As a management team, we will:

1. treat all our staff with respect and dignity

2. ensure equality of opportunity for all

3. maintain a safe and hazard-free working environment

4. maintain confidentiality at all times

5. set high, achievable standards for the organisation

6. deal with inefficiency quickly and competently

7. use resources to the best advantage of clients, staff and the organisation.

As a member of the team, you are expected to:

1. treat everyone with respect and dignity

2. be sensitive and responsive to the needs of others

3. contribute to a safe and hazard-free working environment

4. maintain confidentiality at all times

5. maintain the high quality of the standards we set

6. deal with inefficiency quickly and competently

7. use resources to the best advantage of clients, staff and the organisation

8. participate in staff development opportunities.

- What would you consider to be the benefits of such a values statement to all involved?

- Do you agree with all the points in the list or would you make changes for your own organisation and management teams?

- Why might you want to make changes?

- What else could be usefully included?

Reflect on practice

Does your organisation have a vision, mission and a values statement?
What do they say? Are they still appropriate or are they due for updating? Are they written for everyone? Has everyone seen them? Does everyone own them and believe in them? Do they all work together or are they pulling in opposite directions?

If you have answered no to any of the above questions you will need to spend some time reviewing or developing your statements.

Start with your organisation's vision for the future (or mission statement if you do not have an articulated vision) and put it to the test using the format outlined in Table A.1.

Table A.1 Assessment of an organisation's vision

Vision	Score out of 10	Changes required?
Is it achievable?		
Will it withstand the test of time?		
Is it clearly articulated?		
Is it compatible with service users and staff?		
Is it owned and believed in by everyone?		
Is everyone committed to it?		
Is it inspirational?		
Is it still relevant?		

Developing a vision if your organisation does not have one

Start by imagining where your department or organisation might be in five years' time. To ensure that your vision is achievable, you should also have a good idea about any possible barriers or enhancing factors that could affect the achievement of your vision.

One of the best and simplest ways of finding out about the factors that could influence your vision is to carry out a PEEST analysis:

Political issues
Economic environment
Environmental forces
Social issues
Technological issues

Using each of the headings shown, carry out an analysis of your organisation, and the context in which it operates. This will help you to find out where you are currently, and those factors that could come into play over the next few years.

CASE STUDY — PEEST analysis

Ahmed is carrying out a PEEST analysis to try and help him identify the future of his child care centre in the light of the Children's Centre Initiative in his area.

Political Issues

1. Child care centres are a government issue – no avoiding it

2. Two Surestart centres in the area – 50 child care places each – limited target group only up to 4 years old

Economic Issues

1. Poor area, nursery vouchers used rather than cash

2. Some middle class service users available – mainly use another nursery – why?

3. All nursery competition offer 0 to 5 years service

Social Issues

1. New housing estate being built – could bring in new clients with children

2. More children being born to older parents

3. Single mothers supported by child care costs if they wish to return to learning

4. Lots of children on the streets after school

As Ahmed completes his PEEST analysis, he suddenly realises that he can specialise in child care services that include an out of school club for older children, something none of the other existing services do. A vision for the future is beginning to open up to him.

A.3　The Level 5 leader

Successful organisations have strategic direction that is guided by their vision, mission and company values. These organisations are often led by visionaries who:

- set realistic targets
- champion change
- generate open communication
- know their clients and customers
- empower all employees
- encourage teamwork
- measure and benchmark performance regularly
- strive continually for high standards.

This type of leader is, according to Collins (2001), rather a rare breed. He or she combines a fierce professional will for success with personal humility. When the two are combined, this kind of leader is almost unstoppable.

The first thing to recognise is that the Level 5 leader can be found at any point in the organisation. He or she might be a member of a team responsible to you or based in an administration team, for example. However, when the Level 5 leader is in a position to take an organisation forward or to lead change, he or she frequently demonstrates the ability to take an organisation from good to great.

What if...?
If your organisation had the opportunity to move from the last inspection result you achieved to higher level, what would be the impact on service users, staff, management and owners?

A Level 5 leader clearly shows an ability to appoint people who are good at the job required and good for the organisation (it is usually impossible to split the two). He or she can also usher out people who are in the 'wrong' job, or manoeuvre them into a position that obtains the best possible results for both the client and the organisation.

Collins demonstrates the Level 5 leadership by using the same 'triangle' as in Maslow's Hierarchy. This is illustrated in Figure A.2.

The hierachy can be broken down like this:

Level 1 Highly capable individual
Contributes effectively by using his or her knowledge, skills and good working habits.

Level 2　Contributing team member
Works effectively with others in a group or team setting. Contributes clearly to achievement of team objectives.

Figure A.2 The 5-level hierarchy of leadership

Level 3 Competent manager

Organises people and resources effectively to achieve predetermined objectives, goals and targets.

Level 4 Effective leader

Catalyses commitment and vigorous pursuit of clear and compelling visions. Stimulates the team to achieve high performance.

Level 5 Executive

Builds enduring greatness through personal humility and professional will.

Each of these levels is necessary for the success of the organisation, but, according to Collins, in his book *Great to Good* (2001), the Level 5 leader needs all the skills, knowledge and capabilities of the four lower levels, as well as the special characteristics demonstrated at Level 5.

Characteristics of the Level 5 leader

The Level 5 leader does not take all the credit for what happens within an organisation. He or she makes comments such as "Most of the work for this policy was done by..." or "I can't take the credit for this – we have a marvellous team". In addition, the Level 5 leader:

- never settles for 'good' but constantly strives for 'even better';
- has ambitions only for their organisations, not themselves;
- never blames other people or external factors when something goes wrong;
- maintains a quiet calm;
- acts with determination and unwavering resolve;
- relies on inspired standards for motivation;
- does not rely on their charisma to motivate staff.

CASE STUDY — The Level 5 leader

Janet would like to consider herself a Level 5 leader. She is constantly talking about where she would like her business to be in five years' time. She tells her staff about the benefits of working hard to earn more money for themselves and her shareholders. Her vision is to double the current number of clients by establishing an intermediary care unit, thus increasing the company's income.

She very rarely asks team members about their vision for the organisation, but often asks for feedback about her own. The team tends to find her rather tedious and thinks she is quick to point out errors about the way team members contribute towards the workload and, ultimately, her goal.

Her team is used to the way she works and has found techniques to avoid being on the receiving end of an explosion of temper when something goes wrong. Staff hide any mishaps from her attention whenever possible.

- Is Janet a Level 5 leader?
- How would she need to change to become a true Level 5 leader?

A Level 5 leader would:

- explore trends and changes in his or her area of work to keep the organisation at the cutting edge
- meet with team members and ask them to share their hopes for the future. Acknowledge any commonalities
- disseminate his or her vision widely and ask for feedback. Take action on the feedback, if appropriate
- ask people if they can see their role within the future vision
- include discussions on the future at team meetings or other regular events.

What if...?

If your colleagues were asked to select key words to describe your leadership style, what do you think they would be? Are they words that are closely related to leadership skills and knowledge, or will the words chosen mostly reflect the ability to manage?

Use these key words to reflect upon your own leadership skills. Consider any changes that might be required so that you can meet the standards set by a Level 5 leader.

A.4   The emotionally intelligent leader

The work of Daniel Goleman builds on theories developed in the early 1980s and 1990s and is applied to the workplace. It concentrates on a leader who is capable of managing people with empathy and sensitivity, which he considers should be central to all actions. At the same time, he argues that leaders need to demonstrate an ability to innovate, to be visionaries and to persuade others to their point of view without creating alienation – that is, an ability to lead and inspire teams.

The term 'emotional intelligence' means having the capacity to recognise our own feelings as well as the feelings of others. It also means being able to recognise our own motivational needs and those of others. Goleman recognises that it is possible to be academically intelligent but emotionally unintelligent.

Golman uses five emotional and social competencies to help define the emotionally intelligent leader. These are:

Self-awareness
- knowing our feelings and using them to guide decision making
- being aware of our own abilities
- having well grounded self confidence.

Self-regulation
- not allowing emotions to interfere with the task required
- being conscientious
- having a sense of deferred gratification
- coping well with, and recovering quickly from, emotional distress.

Motivation
- using deepest preferences to guide towards goals and targets
- striving to improve
- persevering with barriers and setbacks.

Empathy
- knowing what people are feeling
- seeing things from the perspective of others
- cultivating rapport with a wide range of people.

Social skills
- handling emotions well
- accurately reading social or work situations
- interacting smoothly
- negotiating well and having the ability to settle conflicts
- using this knowledge and skill to persuade others.

It might be assumed that women prove to be the most emotionally intelligent leaders as they are generally better at interpersonal skills than men. However, men can also be emotionally intelligent leaders. Goleman feels that emotional intelligence can be learned, just like any other management skill or technique.

Goleman has also applied the theory of emotional intelligence to the performance of teams. He noted that 'star' teams display emotionally intelligent behaviour. For example:

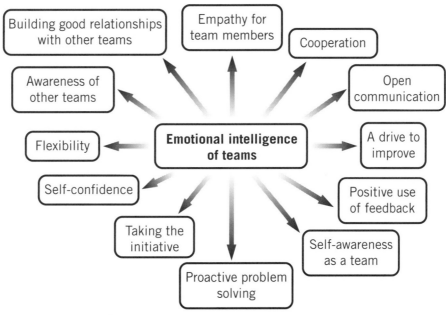

Figure A.3 Factors influencing the emotional development of teams

CASE STUDY – Emotionally intelligent leadership

Elaine is a carer. She has recently gone through a traumatic divorce and is now living on her own with two young sons, aged 8 and 11. The school holidays are coming up and there is nobody to assist with her childcare. Elaine has come to her manager, Mike, to discuss the possibilities available to her. She is rather aggressive and demanding.

Mike is sympathetic to her problem. He recognises that the aggression is a result of anxiety about the school holidays. He quickly tells Elaine that he is sure something can be arranged, and that she has his full support. He will investigate the possibilities and get back to her by the end of the following day.

The next day, Mike calls Elaine into his office. He suggests that she could reduce the hours of her working day to enable her to take the children to and from school. She can also take five weeks' unpaid leave during the summer holidays, spread across the whole year so that she will still have a salary each month. The money saved will be used pay part-time staff to cover her remaining duties.

- How is Mike an emotionally intelligent leader?
- What employment law did he invoke to aid his decision?
- What might be the outcome of his decision for both the organisation and Elaine?
- What would you have done?

A.5

The fundamentals of exemplary leadership

Colleen Wedderburn Tate (1999) explored the issues around leadership in nursing and came up with a list of five characteristics demonstrated by the 'exemplary leader'. These were:

Inspiring a shared vision: Leaders have a desire to see things done differently. They are able to communicate with others to develop a shared vision and a common goal.

Modelling the way: Exemplary leaders are good role models. They set examples of good practice. They are always willing to do anything that they might ask of others. Evaluation of work in progress is a central part of their role, with corrective action taken as necessary.

Challenging the process: Innovation is encouraged along with devolved decision-making. Exemplary leaders are willing to take calculated risks. Staff are supported when they make mistakes. Trial and error is seen as part of learning.

Encouraging the heart: Morale is maintained by the leader through the celebration of success; achievement is recognised and praised. There is a visible valuing of all staff, who are always expected to perform well.

Enabling others to act: Exemplary leaders form collaborative relationships. They build teams that work effectively with their clients and customers. Delegation is seen as a method of staff development.

Actions for an exemplary leader to take

- Find ways of encouraging more interaction amongst team members, including yourself.
- Use the word 'we' instead of 'I' to help foster a team spirit.
- Delegate important tasks to others, providing support along the way.
- Regularly visit team members in their place of work.
- Admit your mistakes.
- Celebrate success by praising often and openly.
- Stimulate and energise the team by providing non-routine work for people who only follow routine tasks.

It is clear that a leader of the 21st century needs to combine a range of skills and knowledge to meet the more human aspects of their work. Managing by systems and processes alone is no longer sufficient; we need to lead through humility, professional will and a sincere desire for success.

A.6   Ways of developing yourself

There are four major ways that you can use to develop yourself and your leadership skills and knowledge. These are:

- trial and error;
- observation of others;
- academic learning;
- reflective practice.

Trial and error

This is often known as 'learning by your mistakes' but there is really is no substitute for experience. You need to challenge yourself: always doing routine tasks will not stretch your ability or allow you to learn and develop. You can read extensively about chairing meetings but it is only when you actually do it that you will have the opportunity to develop your skills.

Observation of others

Other people can be an excellent source of personal development. Look around you for role models and good coaches. These could be people you work with, or people you have read about or seen on television. Many people, famous and infamous, have been regarded as good leaders in the past – find out about them.

Academic learning

This includes reading or taking courses but also try attending workshops or seminars. If you cannot be away from the workplace easily, try distance learning.

Reflective practice

Schon (1983) suggested that professionals who have to carry out complex tasks often develop by reflecting on their experiences and then testing out new ideas in their daily work routines. Reflective learning is a continuous cycle that is a way of thinking rather than just problem solving.

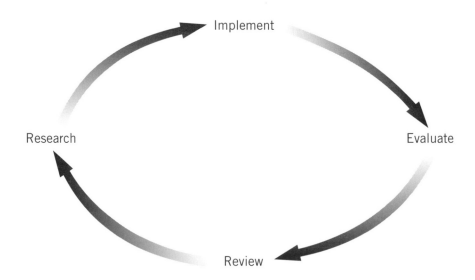

Figure A.4 The cycle of reflective learning

A reflective practitioner needs to have three basic attitudes towards the practice of reflexivity. They are:

- a willingness to question – what and why, implications;
- open-mindedness – listen, look, research, recognise;
- whole-heartedness – honesty, self-awareness, internal strength.

Styles of learning

People like to learn in different ways. The three main styles of learning are:

- visual (seeing);
- kinaesthetic (doing);
- auditory (listening).

You need to understand your own preferred method of learning so that you can plan for your continuing development in the best way possible. It is likely that most of us use each of the different methods of learning to some degree. However, we will probably have a preference for one style over another. The way you choose to learn will need to match your preferred learning style.

Finding your preferred learning style(s)

Read the statements in the left-hand column of Table A.2, then complete each sentence by putting a tick in the box that best suits you. Then add up the number of ticks in each column to see which style you prefer the most.

Table A.2 Defining preferred learning styles

When you spell, you ...	visualise the word or write it down	'sound out the word'	write down the word to 'feel' it
When you are imagining something, you ...	see vivid pictures in your mind	think of sounds you might hear	think of what it would feel like
When you concentrate, you ...	have to clear clutter from around you	hate being distracted by external noise	need to move around and perhaps talk to yourself
When you are angry, you ...	become silent and seethe	demonstrate it through outbursts of noise or words	storm off and slam the door
When you forget something, you ...	forget names but remember faces and places	forget faces and places but remember names	try to remember what you did and the places you actually visited
When you contact someone to make a request, you ...	prefer face to face	prefer the telephone	rehearse what you are going to say
When you praise someone, you ...	give them a note	tell them to their face	give them a pat on the back or a hug
When you try to interpret someone's mood, you ...	look at their facial expression	listen to their tone of voice	watch their body movements
When you are reading, you ...	like description best	like dialogue best	like a strong storyline with plenty of action. You may not like reading at all
When you are training, you ...	prefer demonstrations, slides and diagrams	like verbal explanations, lectures and talks	like role play, practical work and active tasks
When you are having a conversation, you ...	dislike listening for too long	enjoy listening to others but are keen to talk too	gesture a lot and use expressive movements
If you had a choice of career, you would ...	want to be an artist or photographer	want to be a musician	want to be a sports personality

Each column represents a different style of learning:

Column 1   Visual learner
Column 2   Auditory learner
Column 3   Kinaesthetic learner

You could also use the chart with members of staff as part of their induction or appraisal process. Once you know a preferred learning style, you can choose the method most appropriate for you or your staff.

Developing a personal action plan

The next stage in your personal development is to recognise those areas that you want to develop. Having read about the Level 5 leader, for example, you may want to develop particular skills and qualities that will enable you to reach this goal, or you may want to collect some more information about leadership. There is an enormous amount of related information available to you.

Use the action plan below to help you think through the process in a planned and coherent way.

Table A.3 Development action plan

Current practice	Goal for improvement	Completion date	Measure of success	Support required	Resources required

Make as many copies as you require or, alternatively, create your own chart.

Key leadership words

Throughout this section, we have found the same words being used again and again by a range of management and leadership theorists. They all have certain things or views in common with each other. They all agree that the following aspects of leadership are central to the whole process:

- vision
- aspiration
- inspiration
- motivation
- communication
- empathy and feelings.

The true leader of the 21st century uses all of these qualities to develop positive working relationships with people central to their core business. In health and social care, this means both clients and staff. If we are to be inspirational leaders, we have a duty to care about our staff as well as our clients.

There is no doubt that the successful leader of the 21st century has a demanding role. However, they also have a fulfilling and worthwhile job. It should be possible to enjoy your leadership, to be able to look back in five years time and think about all those people you have enabled to go forward into their own careers. You should be able to be proud of your achievements, knowing that others are proud to have worked alongside you.

Useful references for Leaders

Chellen, S. (2003) *The Essential Guide to the Internet for Health Professionals*. London: Routledge.

Collins, J. (2001) *Good to Great*. London: Random House Business Books.

Goleman, D. (1999) *Working with Emotional Intelligence*. London: Bloomsbury Publishing.

Hannagan, T. (1998) *Management: Concepts and Practices*. Harlow: FT Prentice Hall.

Heller, R. and Hindle, T. (1998) *DK Essential Manager's Manual*. London: Dorling Kindersley.

Schon, D. A. (1983) *How Professionals Think in Action*. New York: Basic Books.

Wedderburn Tate, C. (1999) *Leadership in Nursing*. London: Churchill Livingstone.

Useful Website

Health Service Journal
www.hsj.co.uk

How to recruit team members successfully

- ■ B.1 Introduction to the recruitment process
- ■ B.2 The legal requirements in the recruitment process
- ■ B.3 Job descriptions and person specifications
- ■ B.4 Shortlisting
- ■ B.5 Interviewing

B.1 Introduction to the recruitment process

This section explores the knowledge base skills and legal procedures that you, as manager, will be required to demonstrate to attract the calibre of staff necessary to deliver qualitative care.

The recruitment process is by no means static; it is always fluid, as team members move on to occupy new positions, resign, or simply retire. Therefore it becomes imperative to have in place both recruitment and selection processes that retain that dynamic appeal in order to assist in the successful employment of desirable team members.

It must ensure for appropriate gender, age, race and skills match, as well as required national standards of competence to the Care Standards Act 2000 in order to reflect your commitment to building and inspiring your team.

- What are the basic ground rules in the event of a vacancy?
- What are the prerequisite procedures needed to recruit and simultaneously comply with legal procedures?

If your practice setting has a vacancy, it will be helpful to ask some basic questions before seeking to fill that position:

- What type of job do I need to advertise, for example, full time, part time, and so on?
- Will the title remain the same?
- Does the setting still require this role?
- Does the role meet its stated purposes or need adapting?

Ideally, if it is a role focusing upon meeting service user needs, then proactive consideration of under-represented groups should be actioned to include people with disabilities, people of an ethnic minority or male staff.

The above questions and subsequent answers form the basis of your required job analysis. Best practice dictates three specific methods of undertaking that job analysis before attempting to fill a vacancy.

- Interview the person leaving the position, as well as other team members. Combined, their knowledge of the post and its status may offer valuable information about retention, change and review.
- Review previous appraisals of post holder. This information will focus upon performance and its actual interrelationship to organisational needs.
- Review and study team members' profiles. The staff profile offers an insight into both actual performance and attainment whilst in the post, and its continuing usefulness.

These three simple methods, which underpin your job analysis, are based on consultation and review. Always ensure before beginning the recruitment process that it is undertaken to consider the nature of the actual post, set against changing service user needs.

Additionally, proactive discussion with fellow team members encourages a stakeholder culture of ownership, responsibility and accountability to the recruitment process.

This supports the whole notion of leading and inspiring teams whatever the setting or specialism.

What if...?

If a vacancy arose in your practice setting, why might a job analysis be pertinent before beginning the recruitment process, and why might it be productive?

Reflect on practice

What ground rules do you have in place that might inform the recruitment process when team-based vacancies arise?

CASE STUDY — Persistent vacancy

You have a long-term vacancy for a care enabler within a specialised unit for adults with multiple physical disabilities. In order to speed up the process of recruitment:

- consider undertaking a job analysis
- focus on appropriate role change and why
- think about the methods of consultation you might utilise and with whom you might consult
- ask yourself whether a team-based stakeholder culture would be constructive to meeting the recruitment needs of your practice setting.

Having put in place the ground rules to follow in the event of a vacancy, it now becomes necessary to put in place the procedures to recruit legally and to:

- understand the legal requirements involved in the recruitment process
- write the job description and person specification
- advertise the position
- form the selection panel and explain its duties
- see the importance of shortlisting (shortlist form sampler included on page 196)
- focus on the interviewing environment
- understand the process of a managed interview (sampler form of an interview form included for demonstration purposes on page 199)
- realise the importance of references
- use interview satisfaction forms (sampler copy included on page 201)
- realise the importance of exit interviews
- realise the importance of dealing with complaints (complaints questionnaire for demonstration purposes included on page 203).

These procedures represent the pathway for recruiting within a legal framework based on retention of team members, hence the thoroughness of both process and practice to recruit successfully.

B.2 The legal requirements in the recruitment process

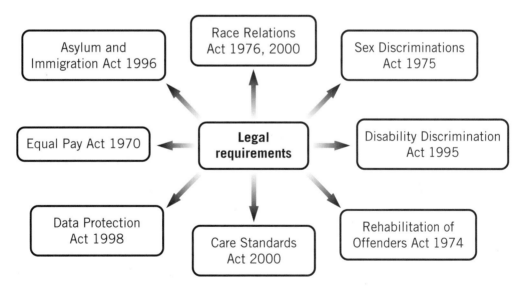

Figure B.1 Legal requirements in the recruitment process

Whilst the legal requirements may be partially explained diagrammatically, the specific context and detail of these Acts and their implication for recruitment of potential and actual staff can be found in Chapter 1, 'Principles and policy' (Section 1.3, 'Equal opportunities legislation and its relationship to work, training and development', pages 18–21).

With a knowledge of the essential legal issues involved in the successful recruitment of team members, the manager must now take responsibility for the writing of accurate job descriptions and person specifications.

B.3 Job descriptions and person specifications

Proactive recruitment demands the drafting of these two basic documents in consultation with all relevant staff. The job description explains the duties and responsibilities required to perform the advertised role. It must be carefully worded to ensure it legally represents the duties and subsequent responsibilities of the actual post and not a hypothetical or ideal post that the manager may have in mind.

Two examples of relevant job descriptions: deputy manager (figure B.2) and manager (figure B.3) are shown below. Both examples are representative of good recruitment practice.

OUTLINE JOB DESCRIPTION

TITLE: Deputy Manager
BASE: Educational Skills Unit
103 Holyhead Road, Coventry, CV1 3AD
RESPONSIBLE TO: Manager – Educational Skills Unit
PRIMARY PURPOSE: To support the manager in the management of the Educational Skills Unit, its staff team and other resources, in an efficient and cost effective manner, so as to create an environment in which each client is able to derive the most benefit from their attendance.

* * * * * * *

PRINCIPAL RESPONSIBILITIES:

1. To work with the Manager in the management of the Educational Skills Unit, within the terms of Coventry City Council's registration requirements, the philosophy of care for the Educational Skills Units and within Broad View Care's practices and procedures.

2. **The Clients**
   a) To be aware of the needs of each client (physical, psychological, social, spiritual and sexual).
   b) To assist each client in respect of dressing, bathing, toileting, mobility, minor dressings, nursing and other self help skills.
   c) To establish a working care plan for each client that takes into account their identified needs, their wishes where expressed, their skills and aspirations. Realistic goals and objectives are to be agreed for – and, where possible, with – each client.
   d) To monitor on an ongoing basis care plans, update and amend as necessary.
   e) To explore – and implement – opportunities for each client to develop their social skills.

f) To explore – and implement – opportunities for each client to develop their personal/domestic skills.

g) To liaise closely with the relatives of each client.

h) To liaise closely with other clinical services e.g. Speech Therapy, Clinical Psychology in respect of each client.

i) To liaise closely with the Home Manager of each client.

3. Staff

In partnership with the Manager and in her absence take lead responsibility:-

a) To ensure that the Educational Skills Unit is adequately and appropriately staffed at all times.

b) To manage all subordinate staff at the Educational Skills Unit.

c) To assist in the recruitment of new staff at the Educational Skills Unit.

d) To participate in induction training for all new staff at the Educational Skills Unit.

e) To work with Care Assistant staff – as part of the staff personal development programme – in setting key objectives; identifying training needs and providing appropriate training opportunities.

f) To undertake counselling of staff where necessary.

g) To be aware of Broad View Care's disciplinary procedure; seek advice from the Manager – and in her absence from the Directors – in the event of possible need to implement the procedure.

h) To ensure that all staff are aware of fire procedures, health and safety and food hygiene regulations.

i) To maintain records and manage staff sickness and annual leave.

4. The Building

a) To ensure that high standards of cleanliness and tidiness at the Educational Skills Unit are maintained at all times.

b) To ensure that all fire fighting equipment at the Educational Skills Unit is regularly checked, maintained and the maintenance is duly recorded.

c) To undertake periodic health and safety checks within the Educational Skills Unit, drawing any deficiencies to the immediate attention of the manager.

d) To ensure that the general fabric of the Educational Skills Unit is maintained at a high standard, keeping a record of repairs/maintenance needed/undertaken and drawing any problems/deficiencies to the immediate attention of the Manager.

5. Personal

a) To identify own training needs and agree key objectives with the Manager as part of staff personal development.

b) To work with the manager and staff in projecting a positive image of the Educational Skills Unit within the community.

c) To propose ideas and initiatives to the manager for continuing to improve the services of the Educational Skills Unit.

d) To keep up to date with professional practices within this field.

6. Financial

In partnership with the manager and in her absence take lead responsibility:-

a) To practise good financial management, within the agreed budget for the Educational Skills Unit.

b) To ensure that proper financial procedures and records are maintained in respect of residents' monies and petty cash.

c) To explore and promote fund raising initiatives, liaising as necessary with Broad View Care's Fundraiser.

d) To action any recommendations/requirements identified in annual financial audits, undertaken by the Consultant for Management.

7. To attend all visits by the Inspection Officer of Coventry City Council; work with the manager in actioning any recommendations resulting from the visits.

8. In the absence of the manager to deal with any complaints in respect of the Educational Skills Unit; discuss as necessary with the Director for Care.

9. Any other duties as may be delegated by the Manager.

NB: This is an Outline Job Description only and may be amended from time to time in discussion and following agreement with the post holder.

JD Deputy Manager ESU
August 2001

(Used with the kind permission of Broad View Care Limited)

Figure B.2 Job description for deputy manager

OUTLINE JOB DESCRIPTION

TITLE: Manager

BASE: Educational Skills Unit
103 Holyhead Road, Coventry, CV1 3AD

RESPONSIBLE TO: (1) Director for Care, for care/quality matters
(2) Director for Management, for administrative/financial matters

PRIMARY PURPOSE: To manage 109 Holyhead Road, its staff team and other resources, in an efficient and cost effective manner, so as to create an environment in which each resident is able to lead as full and as happy a life as possible.

∗ ∗ ∗ ∗ ∗ ∗ ∗

PRINCIPAL RESPONSIBILITIES:

1. To manage 109 Holyhead Road within the terms of Coventry City Council's small homes registration requirements, the philosophy of care for the home and within Broad View Care's practices and procedures.

2. **The Residents**
   a) To be aware of the needs of each resident (physical, psychological, social, spiritual and sexual).
   b) To assist each resident in respect of dressing, bathing, toileting, mobility, minor dressings, nursing and other self help skills.
   c) To establish a care plan for each resident, that takes into account their identified needs, their wishes where expressed, their skills and aspirations. Realistic goals and objectives are to be agreed for – and, where possible, with – each resident.
   d) To monitor on an ongoing basis care plans, update and amend as necessary.
   e) To explore – and implement – opportunities for each resident to develop their social skills, e.g. visits to local shops, pubs, etc.
   f) To explore – and implement – opportunities for each client to develop their personal/domestic skills, ie assisting in general cleanliness of the home, keeping their bedroom tidy, etc.
   g) To liaise closely with the relatives of each resident, encouraging them to visit the home and to involve themselves in their care.
   h) To liaise closely with the local GP, dentist and other professional staff in respect of each resident.
   i) To liaise closely with the day care manager of each resident.

3. **Staff**
   a) To ensure that the home is adequately and appropriately staffed at all times.
   b) To manage all subordinate staff at the home.
   c) To be responsible for the recruitment of new staff in the home.
   d) To arrange induction training for all new staff in the home.
   e) To work with each member of staff – as part of the staff personal development programme – in setting key objectives; identifying training needs and providing appropriate training opportunities.
   f) Liaise with Broad View Care's Training and Development Manager in the organisation and provision of training courses.
   g) To undertake counselling of staff where necessary.
   g) To be aware of Broad View Care's disciplinary procedure; seek advice from the Directors in the event of possible need to implement the procedure.
   h) To ensure that all staff are aware of fire procedures, health and safety and food hygiene regulations.
   i) To maintain records and manage staff sickness and annual leave.

4. The Building

a) To ensure that high standards of cleanliness and tidiness at the home are maintained at all times and to maintain homeliness.

b) To ensure that all fire fighting equipment in the home is regularly checked, maintained and that the maintenance is duly recorded.

c) To undertake periodic health and safety checks within the home, drawing any deficiencies to the immediate attention of the Director for Care.

d) To ensure that the general fabric of the home is maintained to a high standard, keeping a record of repairs/maintenance needed/undertaken and drawing any problems/deficiencies to the immediate attention of the Director for Care.

5. Personal

a) To identify own training needs and agree key objectives with the Directors as part of staff personal developments.

b) To work with the Directors and staff in projecting a positive image of the home within the community.

c) To propose ideas and initiatives to the Directors for continuing to improve the services of the home.

d) To keep up to date with professional practices within this field and, if appropriate, maintain registration and PREP.

6. Financial

a) To practise good financial management, within the agreed budget for the Educational Skills Unit.

b) To ensure that proper financial procedures and records are maintained in respect of residents' monies and petty cash.

c) To explore and promote fund raising initiatives, liaising as necessary with Broad View Care's Fundraiser.

d) To action any recommendations/requirements identified in annual financial audits, undertaken by the Director for Management.

7. To attend all visits by the Inspection Officer of the small homes unit of Coventry City Council; to work with the Directors in actioning any recommendations resulting from the visits.

8. To deal with any complaints in respect of the home; discuss as necessary with the Director for Care.

9. Any other duties as may be delegated by the Directors.

NB: This is an Outline Job Description only and may be amended from time to time in discussion and following agreement with the post holder.

JD Manager HR
August 2001

(Used with the kind permission of Broad View Care Limited)

Figure B.3 Job description for manager

The person specification remains a completely different document as it goes beyond mere description and represents an analysis of the main characteristics required to perform the advertised job to the stated standard. The specification contained in this document provides the basis upon which all questions at interview are asked. It is of paramount importance to ensure both accuracy and relevance in all published wording.

The manager will be faced with a choice of formats when completing the person specification. Perhaps the simplest and most broadly used is the Alec Rodgers Seven Point Plan, which was written and accredited by the National Institute of Industrial Psychology in 1970.

The Rodgers specification is shown in figure B.4.

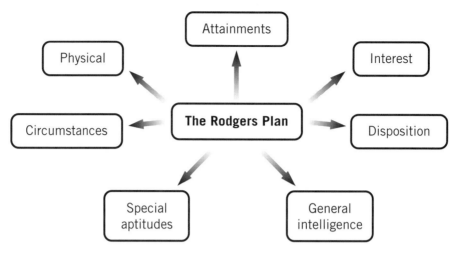

Figure B.4 The Rodgers Seven Point Plan

These particular seven points will assist writers who are preparing a detailed summary required for a potential candidate to occupy any position within the care sector. A point of note is to differentiate between 'essential' and 'desirable' qualities for each criterion. This is demonstrated below in an example of a person specification for a support worker involved in the care of children with a physical disability.

Table B.1 A person specification for a support worker

	Attribute	Essential	Desirable
1	**Physical**	Physically fit	None
2	**Attainments**	Minimum NVQ 2 in Childcare	Willingness to participate to NVQ 3 and above
3	**General intelligence**	Quick thinker	Alert at all times
4	**Special aptitudes**	• Excellent oral communication skills • Experience of working with people with a physical disability • Ability to encourage service users' ability to advocate their needs • Ability to work in a team and autonomously as required • Ability to liaise with service users' families and other significant persons	Ability to learn new skills to maximise user mobility and independence
5	**Interests**	• To possess a genuine interest in promoting both the care and support of physically disabled persons in their daily lives • Ability to work with people of all ages, race, gender and ethnic origin without prejudice	Participate in directed activities that will improve quality of life for physically disabled people

6	Disposition	• Maintain a sense of humour • Ability to resolve problems and work in a team with varied work patterns • Demonstrate a commitment to developing anti-discriminatory practice and equal opportunities in own personal working practices	Person-centred in all work practices
7	Circumstances	Ability to undertake a split shift system of work as well as to work weekends in rotation	Maintain a flexible attitude to different work practices to meet user needs at all times

The principal advantage of employing the Seven Point Plan rests upon its ability to maintain fair and objective criteria relevant to the advertised post. It must be emphasised that both fairness and objectivity are intrinsic to maintaining equal opportunities throughout the recruitment process.

Reflect on practice

Review the person specification for your personal work role. Design a person specification using the Alec Rodgers Seven Point Plan to assist in assessing essential characteristics of the role for future interviewing purposes.

CASE STUDY — Creating new job descriptions

You are a newly appointed manager of a community-based project that supports families whose dependants suffer from a mental illness. You discover that many of the existing staff's job descriptions are out of date and no longer relate to many of their current duties. Another concern is that person specifications have either been lost or do not exist. You realise that you must rectify this situation immediately to comply with legal and good employment practices.

• How will you draft new job descriptions for all new posts?

• How will you draft new person specifications for all current positions?

• What forms of consultation might you utilise to achieve the task?

Having written the required job description and person specification, you are now in a position to advertise the post. The specification represents the minimum information you will require when writing a job advertisement to attract new team members.

The starting point consists of:
• A job title.
• A job description: briefly state the principal duties required.

- The organisation's role and purpose: state what work the organisation engages in and why.
- Salary: the rate of pay should be clearly stated.
- Qualifications and experience/Experience: minimum levels of qualifications and experience must be stated.
- Location of both organisation and post: state where these are specifically located.
- How to proceed with an application: give details of a named person and phone number to contact for more information about the post.
- Any special benefits: these benefits would be unique to this employer and might include mileage allowance, bonus payments for weekend work or holiday/bank holiday work, and so on, as well as benefits such as a loyalty payment paid after one full year of consistent employment.

The manner of presentation is important to the reader as it promotes the first impression of job and organisation in unison. It cannot be emphasised enough that part of the Equal Opportunities Commission's role is to monitor, at random, the content and wording of advertisements. Prosecutions might arise if advertisements discriminate on grounds of race, disability, gender or age.

What if...?

If you were asked to write a job description for a senior carer in your private residential home for older people, using the criteria for writing a job description below, identify your considered opinion of the criteria's strengths and weaknesses.

Job title (Senior Carer)	Strengths (Comment)	Weaknesses (Comment)
Job description		
Organisational purpose		
Salary		
Qualification/Experience		
Location of post and organisation		
How to apply (process)		
Special benefits		

With the job advertised, as manager, you will be required to form a selection panel from within your practice setting. The panel may include fellow team members, senior carers, service users, and/or significant others of your choice.

In order to form your selection panel there are certain criteria as manager that you must observe to demonstrate best practice. They include determining the composition of your selection panel to reflect age, race, gender and service user/carer mix. Ensure you negotiate realistic timescales for their preparation and check that each member has a working knowledge of internal recruitment practices, is aware of statutory ACAS advisory guideleines, understands the organisation's equal opportunities policy and procedures, possesses effective oral communication skills, and can make a rational judgement based on presented evidence.

Reflect on practice

In your professional experience, have you ever participated in a selection panel process? Make notes on the kinds of preparation you either undertook or might have undertaken to preserve best practice at this central stage of recruitment.

With preparation and composition negotiated and agreed, it is central to the successful recruitment of team members that selection panels understand their duties. These can be briefly explained as:

- collectively writing the job description
- collectively writing the person specification
- using the person specification to agree questions to be asked at interview
- agreeing upon how questions are to be assessed and weighted
- agreeing upon what information should be sent out to candidates prior to interview, aside from job description and person specification
- drawing up a shortlist
- interviewing all candidates
- considering references
- collectively agreeing a final decision of successful candidate on merit alone
- communicating with the successful candidate: verbally within 24 hours and providing written confirmation within 72 hours.
- agreeing in writing the start date for new appointee
- agreeing that the manager should perform exit interviews, if requested, for unsuccessful candidates for professional developmental purposes.

CASE STUDY — Panel preparation for selection interview

You manage a community home care service for people with learning disabilities. Due to the level of care each service user needs, you have been required to advertise extensively for care enablers and support workers. Prior to any selection interview, you wish to be certain that your panel agrees the criteria for each new position.

- How do you go about agreeing and writing the designated job description and person specification?

- What realistic and manageable timescales might you consider for this purpose?

- What kinds of motivators might you employ to retain commitment from panel members to achieve this task?

- What assessment criteria, drawn from the person specification, would you need to consider?

- How will you agree equal composition of roles to reflect race, age, gender, disability and service user participation?

- What other pre-planning arrangements might you need to consider prior to selection?

B.4 Shortlisting

The shortlisting process commences after the closing date for applications. A panel process is by far fairer in being able to accurately assess candidates' suitability than when the role is delegated to one person. Appropriate composition of panel must be allowed to facilitate gender, race, age, disability and service user representation in any or all decision making, which may serve to reduce the incidence of direct or indirect discrimination. Additionally, service user representation not only validates their life experiences, but also addresses their preferences and wishes to recruit only staff who meet their different and collective needs in context.

Using the person specification as the key document of assessment, the panel can read all the applications together and make informed decisions as to who sufficiently meets all the criteria to be interviewed. Not all applicants will meet the criteria given in the person specification and they might have evidenced very logical reasons for this. Best practice dictates that only in the event of a low response are applicants that partially meet the criteria called for interview. Good employment practice might call for a procedure where all applicants are contacted by letter a week in advance of the interview either inviting them for interview or, if unsuccessful, stating why their application is not being taken further and giving reasons for this. Figure B.5 shows a sampler copy for shortlisting demonstration purposes, which has been designed to uphold best practice in this essential area of recruiting future team members.

SAMPLER COPY ONLY – FOR DEMONSTRATION PURPOSES
SHORTLISTING FORM

CANDIDATE	REQUIRED QUALIFICATIONS	WEIGHTING PROPERTIES: ESSENTIAL (E) IMPORTANT (I) DESIRABLE (D)	REFER BELOW FOR INSTRUCTION	1 2 3 4 5 6 7	COMMENTS AND DECISIONS MADE

NOTE
PERSONNEL CRITERIA   1.1
ONLY USE CRITERIA DRAWN FROM PERSON   1.2
SPECIFICATION   1.3
INDICATE THESE IN RATIO 1 TO 7   1.4
                                                                       1.5
                                                                       1.6
                                                                       1.7

PANEL MEMBER'S SIGNATURE: DATE:

Figure B.5 Sampler shortlisting form

What if...?

If you, as manager, were approached by a service user asking to participate in the selection and recruitment of future staff, how might you respond and in what areas might you advise essential training? Make notes to evidence your response.

CASE STUDY — Selection shortlisting

There has been a recent recruitment drive to employ basic grade, senior care, nursing and managerial staff to run a new purpose-built single storey care home dedicated to supporting people suffering from dementia. This has resulted in some twenty-five applications against a required projected total of nineteen personnel, all of whom meet your stated person specification.

- Given the volume of applications that meet the stated person specification, what additional training might you facilitate for your panel to ensure a fair but desired outcome?

- How will you delegate the different roles that panel members need to occupy?

- What other preparations before or during the shortlisting process might you consider?

- How might you differentiate between strengths and weaknesses of panel members to compensate for the task ahead?

- How might you encourage and empower existing service users to become involved in this process? What methods of motivation might you employ to encourage participation?

With the shortlisting process complete, it now becomes time to focus on the interviewing environment.

B.5　Interviewing

Prior to the interview, it is best practice to select an environment that might give potential candidates the opportunity to represent themselves in the most comprehensive way. What areas require essential attention?

One might focus on an area of the practice setting that ensures minimum disruption. Equally, seating arrangements need to be organised in such a way that any physical barriers are removed, to facilitate the types of engaging conversation required. Question whether the environment itself is distracting: focus on furniture, paint, wall coverings, ventilation, and overuse of pictures (if so, remove). Additionally, the environment has to be accessible to all candidates, whether able bodied or disabled, and reasonable adjustments are required under the auspices of the Disabilty Discrimination Act 1995.

With the interviewing environment resolved and necessary preparation put in place, it now becomes essential to focus on the criteria of a managed interview to fulfil the desired outcome.

Always place emphasis on open-ended questions. This type of questioning encourages all candidates to give a measured response and to be able to draw upon and convey their specific knowledge, skills and different life experiences. Probe where necessary, to allow candidates who become 'frozen' to offer a more detailed response.

Encourage the use of reflective questioning, which both allows and enables candidates to reflect on the actual content of their response. This should allow a much more detailed response. Encourage q candidates to ask questions of their own choosing, pertinent to their application.

Rules in the interviewing process

- Do not allow candidates to divert or bypass questions.
- Do not allow candidates to be disrupted or manipulated.
- Do not allow candidates to repeat themselves; ideally point it out.
- Do not allow candidates too long to reply; each candidate must be given the same time to respond unless a particular and declared disability prevents this.

Interviewing styles

The interviewer must always focus on the questions being asked and the response made, therefore care must be taken to avoid becoming:

- self-opinionated: giving personal opinions and not sticking to the facts
- argumentative: raising tone or pitch of voice, which might be perceived as threatening, only increases the risk of candidate stagnation or, at worst, conflict
- too subjective: where questions lack objectivity and might be perceived as too user friendly or possibly even conveying hidden agendas that candidates may not comprehend.

These styles are to be avoided at all costs; collectively they will fail to elicit the information required to make both accurate and fair judgements.

End of interview

Remind candidates that the recruitment process demands taking up references, ideally two, one of which must be from a recent employer. Ask what period of statutory notice is required by their current employer if the position were to be offered to them. Timescales will vary depending on length of service. Inform each candidate of the timespan before a response, whether offer of employment is made or not. Inform each candidate that a medical examination may be required, subject to his or her own general practitioner's report. Additionally, specify to each candidate the type of exit interview that will be available, if unsuccessful, for professional developmental purposes.

Close of interview

At the end of the interview process, as manager, request each panel member to complete his or her interview form. A sampler form for demonstration purposes only has been designed for guidance (see Figure B.6). It includes a scoring matrix for ease of collation for each question asked.

SAMPLER COPY – FOR DEMONSTRATION PURPOSES ONLY
INTERVIEW FORM

POST ADVERTISED:	WEIGHTING PRIORITY:		RANKING MATRIX FOR QUESTIONS ASKED:					
VENUE:	– ESSENTIAL		A – OUTSTANDING					
DATE:	– IMPORTANT		B – EXCELLENT C – GOOD					
CANDIDATE NAME:	–DESIRABLE		D – SATISFACTORY E – QUESTION NOT ANSWERED					

QUESTIONS ASKED – MUST RELATE TO THE REQUIRED CRITERIA OF PERSON SPECIFICATION ONLY!	WEIGHTING PRIORITY (AS ABOVE)	1	2	3	4	5	6	7
REASONS AND DECISIONS. PLEASE COMMENT. 1 2 3 4 5 6 7								
PANEL MEMBER'S SIGNATURE:					DATE:			

Figure B.6 Sampler interview form

CASE STUDY — Interview review

At the end of every completed set of interviews, it remains imperative that you review your selection criteria to ensure that fairness, objectivity and best practice is demonstrated in each instance.

- How will you evidence that questions used are only relevant to the advertised post?

- In your opinion, what is the optimum number of questions to be asked at interview?

- What values do you place on the role of non-verbal communication, remembering it remains a two-way process?

- What methods might you employ to clarify answers given by applicants to aid collective understanding?

- How might the employment of an independent observer aid both interviewing style and, equally, offer an impartial view of a candidate's response?

- How might you improve questions that are related to both job description and person specification without making an overt reliance on either one?

Before making an offer of employment, it is essential that, as manager, you obtain two references. The first should be from his or her most recent employer and the second might be a previous employer or someone who can confirm the following:

- knowledge of the person and in what capacity
- duties and responsibilities whilst in most recent employment
- professional organisational skills
- reliability
- honesty
- punctuality
- whether the person can function in a team and in what capacity
- overall performance in his or her previous post
- why the referee would recommend this person in particular for this position.

It is always wise to remind the referee of their duty of care to the person and their intended employment.

Reflect on practice

What other information might you seek of a prospective staff member?

What if...?

If you were required to send out a reference request, what types of questions might you ask to their current or past employer? Make a note of your thoughts.

References serve to validate candidates' applications and increasingly have a legal status in protecting both service user and staff interest. There are three key rules of managing the reference process.

1 Do not make an offer of employment before receiving a reference.
2 Do not rely on the content of a verbal reference alone; notions of interpretation, bias and verification may pose future legal problems.
3 Do not rely on the subjective views of character alone; references must always be supported with factual evidence.

Once you have decided to appoint, it is good employment practice to review your selection procedures regularly. This is one way of establishing candidate satisfaction in the overall recruitment process. It must be remembered that staff selection interviews represent a managed event and ideally should be prerehearsed with ascribing roles of chair, interviewer and an observer. Equally, composition reflecting appropriate age, race, gender and disability should serve to bear out the criteria cited in the person specification.

Ideally, an interview satisfaction form should be sent to all candidates as quickly as possible post-interview when the experience is still clear in their minds. An enclosed stamped, addressed envelope is more likely to promote a response. Whilst the content of satisfaction replies is likely to be subjective, it would be wise to acknowledge the relevance of this unique personal experience and to take on board opinions made, to facilitate future change. For reasons of best practice, a sampler copy of an interview satisfaction form has been designed for this purpose.

SAMPLER COPY – FOR DEMONSTRATION PURPOSES ONLY
INTERVIEW SATISFACTION FORM

NAME OF APPLICANT:
POST APPLIED FOR:
CLOSURE DATE:
PLEASE ANSWER THE FOLLOWING QUESTIONS:

1.1 Were you satisfied with the interview environment?
If not, explain why . . . .
. . . .

1.2 Did you feel comfortable with the composition of the interview panel?   Yes/No (delete as appropriate).
In your opinion, could we make improvements? Briefly state how . . . .
. . . .

1.3 Were the questions asked you in line with the requirements of the person specification?   Yes/No (delete as appropriate).
If no, state why . . . .
. . . .

1.4 Did the interviewers give you sufficient time to answer your questions?   Yes/No (delete as appropriate).
If no, state how much time you were actually given per question . . . .
. . . .

1.5 In your opinion, was both the type of questioning and style of interviewing to your personal/professional satisfaction ?
Yes/No (delete as appropriate).   If no, please explain how you felt . . . .
. . . .

1.6 What improvements to the interview process might you recommend? . . . .
. . . .

Thank you for taking the time to complete this questionnaire. Your views will greatly assist us in improving the interview process for future applicants.

Figure B.7 Sampler copy of interview satisfaction form

As part of the process of quantifying and qualifying candidates' satisfaction, exit interviews for personal and professional developmental purposes are essential for unsuccessful applicants. Additionally, this facility promotes greater equality of opportunity for future applications that candidates might wish to make within the care service sector. Care must be taken to accurately identify those areas that candidates did not meet. It is equally important to advise upon what areas of knowledge, skills and experience they might usefully develop for future applications they might choose to make.

Reflect on practice

In your professional experience, have you ever participated in a formal or informal exit interview as an applicant? What positive or negative outcomes did you derive for developmental purposes? Note down your thoughts for future learning,

What if...?

If you were requested to give an exit interview to three internal unsuccessful applicants for a deputy care managers role within your practice setting, how might your feedback leave candidates feeling either demotivated or optimistic about future applications they may choose to make within the company or externally?

With a process of exit interviews in place as an essential part of the overall recruitment process, as manager, you must be aware of the possibility of complaints. This need not be seen as totally negative, as within a culture of self-advocacy complaining can be a constructive learning curve for any organisation and in particular its recruitment practices. Dealing with complaints post-interview does demand a separate process to be put in place. Ideally, a complaints form could be a part of the original documentation sent out to potential applicants, which assists in creating a transparent recruitment culture.

Upon receipt of the form, compare the applicant's reasons for complaining about your decisions with details that were evidenced by essential recording at interview. To proceed, invite a complainant to meet you for a further discussion. Always advise a complainant of their rights to be accompanied and, as manager, you must also ensure you have a witness. At the meeting, ensure appropriate non-verbal communication to demonstrate genuine and unconditional listening skills to satisfy the complainant that their views and opinions are being taken seriously. The evidence provided at this meeting, albeit verbal, may suggest reasons for a re-interview. If not, then, as manager, you must convey valid reasons why this complaint cannot be supported. If no compromise or agreement can be reached, be sure to advise the complainant of their rights to appeal and provide details of the nearest regional ACAS address.

As a point of caution, record all information for a possible arbitration process. Advisedly cooperate with this process.

No recruitment process is perfect and human error can sometimes cause negative outcomes. However, if this process is transparent, understood, has reviewed and followed required policy of equal opportunities and relevant legislation, which polices all recruitment practices, it should pass the acid test of external scrutiny.

A complaint questionnaire (sampler copy) for demonstration purposes is included to guide developmental practice in this area.

SAMPLER COPY – FOR DEMONSTRATION PURPOSES ONLY
COMPLAINTS QUESTIONNAIRE

STAGE 1 – BIOGRAPHICAL DETAILS
FULL NAME:
CONTACT ADDRESS:

CONTACT TELEPHONE NUMBER: DAYTIME: EVENING:
POST APPLIED FOR:
DATE OF ADVERT:

STAGE 2
Please identify your reasons for complaint: Please tick boxes appropriately:

A) VENUE UNSUITABLE   ☐

B) NOT ACCESSIBLE   ☐

C) CONDUCT OF INTERVIEWS   ☐

D) NOT OFFERED THE POSITION   ☐

E) ANY OTHER REASON   ☐

STAGE 3
Do you believe you have been discriminated against on grounds of:

AGE   SEXUALITY

RACE   POLITICAL VIEWS

ETHNICITY   FAMILY COMMITMENTS

DISABILITY   RELIGIOUS PRACTICES

GENDER   ENGLISH A SECOND LANGUAGE

Are there any other grounds for making a complaint? State here:

Please give a more detailed description of your complaint below:

Figure B.8 Sampler copy of complaints questionnaire

In conclusion, the recruitment process remains a series of managed events that must be the subject of constant review and change if it is to successfully recruit new team members. The process described here can be employed generically throughout the care service sector for this same purpose.

References and further reading

- The Alec Rodgers Seven Point Plan, accredited by the National Institute of Industrial Psychology, 1970.
- Two job descriptions reproduced with the kind permission of Broad View Care Ltd, a registered charity that provides residential care and services for adults with learning disabilities.

FURTHER READING

Adair, J. (1988) *The Action Centred Leader*. The Industrial Society.

Anderson, N., Shackleton, V. (1993) *Successful Selection Interviewing*. Oxford: Blackwell.

Kermally, S. (1997) *Management Ideas in Brief*. Oxford: Butterworth-Heinemann; published in association with the Institute of Management Foundation.

Rabey, G. (1994) *In Charge: Supervising for the First Time*. London: Pitman.

Stewart, D. M. (1994) *Handbook of Management Skills*, 2nd edition. Aldershot: Gower.

WEBSITES

http://online.northumbria.ac.uk/central_departments/humanresources/ic/
Policies%20and%20Procedures/rec/policy.htm

www.dhsspsni.gov.uk/hss/governance/ documents/CSCG_proforma.doc

www.socialcareassoc.com/jobs/selecting_staff.htm

Appeasement solution Placatory approach to resolving conflict.

Appraisal A process that measures individual team members' strengths and weaknesses through realistic target setting.

Assertive communication style Where a team member stands up for his or her rights while at the same time recognising the sensitivities of other team members.

Authoritative solution Employing a single solution to resolve conflict, based only on the manager's authority.

Autocratic leadership style Where all decision making rests with the manager.

Avoidance A manager's refusal to resolve conflict situations.

Banking method of control A system that restricts access to the flow of information coming in and going out of an organisation.

Caldicott guardian The staff member responsible for protecting staff and service user information and for maintaining confidentiality of the data system. Also referred to as the data protection officer.

Care Standards Act 2000 Sets out National Minimum Standards for the provision of care of older people in all residential and nursing homes.

Close gap method A management/ organisational response to maintain the continuity of rules and standards in the workplace.

Closed questioning Questions that are likely to result in a yes/no answer.

Consultative approach (to decision making) A democratic approach that requires listening to the views of others and facilitating contributions to ensure a realistic and binding decision.

Control of Substances Hazardous to Health Regulations 1988/2002 (COSHH) Set out a strategy for safety in workplaces when using substances that may be hazardous to health.

Data Protection Act 1998 Requires that all staff and service user identifiable information (data), whether held manually or on computer, is protected in respect of access, recording, retrieval and storage.

Data protection officer See *Caldicott guardian*.

Data protection policy A written document that describes the way an organisation ensures that staff and service user information is protected and secured in a confidential manner.

Democratic leadership style Where the manager actively consults with staff, encourages participation and offers constructive feedback on performance.

Disciplinary procedure A set of rules relating to the management of behaviour at work. See *Oral warning, First formal written warning, Final written warning, Dismissal*.

Dismissal The final stage in the disciplinary procedure. See also *Dismissal without notice*.

Dismissal without notice Restricted to very serious offences, e.g. gross misconduct including theft or physical violence. See also *Dismissal*.

Equal opportunities legislation Laws protecting the basic rights and responsibilities of people including disadvantaged groups.

External working arrangements Where a team identifies one of its members to work with an external source expert, e.g. a speech therapist.

Facilitative approach (to decision making) Focuses on facilitating a collective decision.

Feedback A two-way interaction to ensure the viewpoint of individuals and teams are heard and clarified in order to address mutually agreed outcomes.

Final written warning A written warning given to a staff member who has previously received a first formal warning for poor performance or misconduct. See *Disciplinary procedure*.

First formal written warning A written warning given to a staff member following poor work performance or misconduct. May follow an oral warning. See *Disciplinary procedure*.

Formal supervision Takes place at regular pre-set intervals with an agreed agenda and methods for reaching shared goals.

Framework method An organisational tool to measure whether an employee's work behaviour falls below the minimum level.

Grievance procedure A process that enables staff members to raise concerns about their working practices, work environment or work-related relationships with their employer.

Health and Safety at Work Act 1974 (HASAWA) Key legislation designed to protect workplace safety.

Health and Safety First Aid Regulations 1981 Covers the treatment of minor injuries or provision of immediate medical aid to minimise the consequences of injury in the workplace.

In house training Training that occurs within the care setting environment.

Individual supervision Oldest type of supervision, which focuses on a one-to-one relationship.

Individual support A method of support that addresses the preferred learning styles of reflectors and theorists.

Informal supervision Involves unplanned *ad hoc* meetings with an agenda agreed spontaneously.

Inter-group conflict Teams or individuals, either internal or external to the practice setting, generating discord.

Internal working arrangements Where a team identifies pairs of individuals to work together.

Interpersonal conflict Discord between two or more people.

Interpersonal skills Characterised by a person's own ability to persuade, motivate, negotiate, support, resolve differences and articulate ideas while respecting the value and diversity of all team members.

Intra-personal conflict Involves a disparity of loyalty between individuals that may include the manager and staff member relationships.

Job description Comprehensive statement that clearly identifies the responsibilities and tasks required of a job role.

Laissez-faire **leadership style** Where the manager promotes an autonomous and interdependent staff culture.

Laissez-faire **solution** Simplistic approach to conflict management in which a manager may appear to avoid making or taking decisions to resolve discord. See *Laissez-faire leadership style*.

Management of Health and Safety at Work Regulations 1999 Designed to ensure far stricter compliance of health and safety legislation than previously determined under the Health and Safety at Work Act.

Manual Handling Regulations 1992 Intended to protect employees engaged in manual handling from injury.

Multidisciplinary joint working arrangements Where a residential based care assistant works with a social worker and district nurse in unison to ensure that a resident's care plan is met.

Negotiative approach (to decision making) Focuses upon reconciling conflicting views or ideas and securing a compromise acceptable to the whole team.

Open-ended questioning Questions that allow a person to give a detailed response.

Oppositional communication style A style that directly or indirectly violates the rights of others.

Oral warning A verbal warning given to a staff member following a minor work work-related offence such as poor timekeeping. See *Disciplinary procedure*.

Person specification An analysis of the main characteristics of a job role to be performed to a competent standard.

Reporting of Injuries, Diseases and Dangerous Occurrences 1985/1995 Ensures the reporting of any injury sustained within the workplace.

Risk assessment A process whereby all work-related actions are assessed for potential hazards with an evaluation of risk undertaken.

Selection criteria Pre-set standards against which candidates for a job may be assessed in a fair and objective way.

Self-assessment performance model A five-stage process that enables team members to review objective setting and identify particular learning needs to fulfil required work plans.

Self-development plan Enables the team member to identify personal objectives.

Single authority approach (to decision making) An approach that depends upon the person with the vested interest, knowledge and skills to make an essential decision without consulting others.

Small group supervision A small group of staff with similar needs or caseloads work together to develop their practice, with the care manager offering support, guidance and coordination.

Small group support A method of support that addresses the preferred learning styles of activists, pragmatists and theorists.

Staff development Ongoing, progressional training tailored to meet the professional needs of the staff member in order to occupy current and future roles within the organisation.

Staff induction The process by which a new member of staff is introduced to an organisation.

Staff training Means by which staff can be formally taught new knowledge and skills, and the results evaluated.

Staff training plan A written document that sets out the organisation's training policy.

Submissive communication style A non-communication style whereby a person relinquishes his or her rights before others.

Supervision training Characterised by individual, small group, pair or even team training that can occur as part of normative supervised arrangements.

Supervision Two-way process where the individual practitioner is nurtured to realise his or her ability, performance and organisational goals.

Tandem supervision Involves two experienced workers who supervise each other, with the care manager monitoring and offering advice when required.

Team briefing A forum, whether planned or spontaneous, for conveying essential information to the whole team.

Team building A management tool for developing both individual and collective practices in unison.

Team supervision The whole team comes together to work on specified tasks.

Whole team support A method of support that addresses the preferred learning styles of activists, theorists, pragmatists and reflectors.

Index

Page numbers in talics refer to tables and charts.